D1233586

Electronic Document Delivery

Commission of the European Communities

ELECTRONIC DOCUMENT DELIVERY

The ARTEMIS concept for document
digitalisation and teletransmission

A study prepared for the Directorate-General
Information Market and Innovation, Commission of
the European Communities

by Adrian Norman (Team Leader), Arthur D. Little

Knowledge Industry Publications, Inc.
White Plains, NY and London.

The Communications Library

Electronic Document Delivery: The Artemis concept for document digitalisation and tele-transmission

Published by

Learned Information (Europe) Ltd.	Learned Information Inc.
Besselsleigh Road	The Anderson House
Abingdon	Stokes Road
Oxford OX13 6LG	Medford, N.J. 08055
England	U.S.A.

U.S. edition published by
Knowledge Industry Publications, Inc.
701 Westchester Avenue
White Plains, N.Y. 10604

Publication arranged by:
Commission of the European Communities,
Directorate-General Information Market and Innovation, Luxembourg

Library of Congress Cataloging in Publication Data

Norman, Adrian R. D.
    Electronic document delivery.

    (Communications library)
    1. Data transmission systems. 2. Facsimile
transmission. 3. Digital communications.
I. Arthur D. Little ltd. II. Title.
III. Title: ARTEMIS concept for document digitalisa-
tion and teletransmission. IV. Series.
TK5105.N67   384.1 '4   81-20774
ISBN 0-86729-011-0   AACR2

This edition published in the United States of America.

10   9   8   7   6   5   4   3   2   1

PREFACE

During the last six years, when Euronet became established, the Commission of the European Communities has initiated more than a hundred studies which are more or less closely related to Euronet, amongst them the ARTEMIS study. I dare say the ARTEMIS study belongs to those few which have the greatest consequences, others being the call for proposals for demonstrations in the field of electronic delivery of primary documents, published in the Official Journal of the European Communities, C 184, 22 July 1980, and then the exhibition and workshop on electronic delivery of primary documents (18/19 December 1980 in Luxembourg) at which manufacturers presented their relevant equipment and services. The proceedings of the workshop will be published during the first half of 1981.

For all that, this result could not be foreseen in December 1979 when we commissioned the ARTEMIS study. Quite early on the Commission realised that Euronet had to be backed up by a fast document delivery service. In 1978 we commissioned the Franklin study which concluded that documents should be ordered electronically in order to do away with postal delays, at least in one direction. But the Franklin Report also dealt with copyright, an issue which soon provoked a dispute between publishers and librarians resulting in a stoppage of all further development of document delivery within the framework of Euronet, with one exception: the parties involved and the Committee advising the Commission on IDST policy questions could agree to the Commission undertaking a purely technical study on document digitalisation and teletransmission provided that it did not touch on the copyright issue. Ergo ARTEMIS.

The copyright issue is now being investigated in parallel and will be discussed at another workshop, probably in Autumn 1981.

Carlo Vernimb
Directorate-General XIII
Commission of the European Communities

ABSTRACT

This report describes a document delivery service, code name ARTEMIS, which prints out on readers' terminals the pages of scientific and technical documents requested from computer data bases.

Source documents are 'digitalised', that is, converted to computer readable form, either as text or as facsimile. The former can be printed on a teleprinter, but does not preserve all the format of the original; the latter can be delivered to a facsimile receiver.

The digitalised documents are stored in data bases attached to host computers. From these, they can be retrieved in response to a user's request and sent overnight via Euronet or another tele-communications network to the user's unattended terminal or to his computer for later printing.

ARTEMIS is a marketplace where information providers and users meet. It should be an open system, with thousands of users and many hosts and data bases, all conforming to standards which make interworking possible. Nevertheless, few of these standards are exclusive to ARTEMIS, which merely promotes existing standardisation efforts.

The study leading to this report was undertaken by management consultants from ADL. They investigated the feasibility of the system and concluded that all the necessary technology exists already. Legal, management and regulatory issues appear to be surmountable, so ADL has recommended to CEC DG XIII that technical trials be started. Meanwhile, agreement must be sought on the proper protection of intellectual property – an issue outside the scope of ADL's study.

Foreword

Electronic delivery of the full text of a document, accomplished at the push of a button, has been an elusive dream of those who deal in information since computers first began to be applied to the publishing and printing process. This report shows that electronic delivery of scientific and technical literature is technically possible today. It tells how one converts a document into a digital form (either text or facsimile) which can be stored in a computer data base and transmitted, via telecommunications, to a printer convenient to a user.

The focus of this account is a description of ARTEMIS (Automatic Retrieval of Text from Europe's Multinational Information Service). ARTEMIS is conceived as the delivery service supplementing DIANE (Direct Information Access Network for Europe), the European information service available through Euronet. Like a library, ARTEMIS would accept information from a provider/publisher when it is available, and deliver it to the user when he wants it. It could print out, overnight, on reader's terminals, the pages of scientific and technical documents requested from computerized data bases.

The European Space Agency is testing the feasibility of ARTEMIS with a pilot project, APOLLO (Article Procurement with On-Line Ordering); in addition, a consortium of British publishers is studying the possiblities of putting a collaborative data base on the Euronet/DIANE system.[1]

The report you are reading was undertaken by Arthur D. Little for the Directorate General of the Commission of the European Communities and published in England by Learned Information. It is divided into two parts (each with its own table of contents). The first reports on the feasibility and possibilities of instant access to full text scientific and technical information. It begins when a fulfillment center (i.e., library) receives a request for a document. Today, the document must be sent through the postal service or by messenger—the first option often precarious and time-consuming; the second, costly. The study then shows, step by step, the technical solutions to this problem, draws the likely development of ARTEMIS, and raises probable legal, regulatory and management issues. The second part (see contents page 83) is a mini-textbook, providing an easily understood technological review of capture and conversion techniques, storage devices, intelligent copiers, printers, document quality, telecommunications and satellite communications. It includes:

- the differences among word processing, text processing and photocomposition;

- an overview of optical character recognition and scanning technologies;
- the types, prices and manufacturers of facsimile equipment, and a list of facsimile networks;
- suppliers of archival storage systems;
- how the user can store and exchange data (via charge-coupled devices (CCDs), floppy discs, digital tape, etc.);
- kinds of intelligent copiers;
- printing technologies; and
- a valuable discussion about the roles of the author, the editor, the compositor and the printer under current and future electronic systems.

This book shows U.S. publishers, librarians, information scientists, data processing specialists and others concerned with the flow of information just how the weak link in the otherwise growing online scientific and technical information publishing industry may be mended. (Note that full-text online services are rare; even basic book and document ordering systems are fledgling. Not a single scholarly journal is accessible online in full text form.) Given the enormous demand for timely information and rising costs for the thousands of scientific and technical journals now published in the U.S., the often promised revolution in information processing and distribution is bound to come. The question is when and how.

F.W. Lancaster notes "There seems little doubt that the cost of producing and distributing publications in electronic form will continue to decline rapidly relative to the costs of publication and distribution in print on paper form."[2] He puts us at the middling stage of a four phase transition from paper to electronics: paper only, dual mode (e.g., *Chemical Abstracts* exists in both printed and machine-readable forms), new electronic only (publications which never existed previously as print on paper and never will be issued as print on paper, e.g., many data bases and data banks), and conversion from paper to electronic.

Electronic document delivery can take its place alongside such information technologies as electronic mail and electronic messaging, facsimile, demand publishing and computerized conferencing, and we can watch these areas closely. There are not many successful examples of these, and a very few examples of electronic document delivery—which really would be a revolution—in the U.S. The National Library of Medicine is developing an experimental system for electronic scanning and storage of documents in biomedicine, and their subsequent retrieval and transmission for interlibrary loan.[3] Studies have been made by the Library of Congress and the National Science Foundation. But we are admittedly at such an early stage of development that the ARTEMIS project described in this book provides the first in depth and full-scale investigation.

Of course, more questions can be raised than can be answered at this stage. The technology is far from completely developed and in place. Once it is, who will control distribution and access? Can electronic document delivery be implemented without major governmental subsidies? How much will it cost? How much information is really needed "instantly"? How long before it becomes economical for at least some sectors of the scientific and business worlds? What happens to copyright protections? How will libraries change? How will publishers react? What new markets will open? Will the equipment be reliable and easy to use? When and how will standardized systems emerge? Publishers, authors, librarians and readers eagerly await new developments.

Ellen A. Lazer, Senior Editor
Knowledge Industry Publications, Inc.
November 1981

Notes

1. *Electronic Publishing—An Introductory Guide* (London: The Publishers Association, 1981), p. 11.
2. F.W. Lancaster, "The Future of the Library in the Age of Telecommunications," in *Telecommunications and Libraries*, by Donald W. King, F.W. Lancaster and Brigitte L. Kenney, et al. (White Plains, NY: Knowledge Industry Publications, Inc., 1981).
3. George R. Thoma, "Compression Techniques for Document Storage and Transmission," *Proceedings of the 43rd ASIS Annual Meeting* 17 (White Plains, NY: Knowledge Industry Publications, Inc., 1980).

TABLE OF CONTENTS

xi

TABLE OF CONTENTS (Continued)

LIST OF TABLES

LIST OF FIGURES

MANAGEMENT SUMMARY

In August 1979, Arthur D Little (ADL) was commissioned by Directorate General XIII (DG XIII) of the Commission of the European Communities (CEC to study 'Document Digitalisation and Teletransmission'. The study confirmed that it is technically possible to convert a document into a digital form which can be stored in a computer data base and transmitted by digital tele-communications to printers located near to those who wish to read the documents.

The cost of digitalisation and teletransmission countinues to fall. However, expensive equipment is required, and large volumes of documents must be handled to achieve low units costs. An operation planned on a European scale could deliver documents overnight at a marginal cost per page which is comparable with the charges made by fulfilment centres now meeting requests by copying and mailing documents.

ADL conceived a system, called ARTEMIS, which would use existing technology in a new way and looked at the organisational, managerial, legal and regulatory issues involved in establishing it as a Europe-wide operation.

ARTEMIS is the name of the Greek goddess equivalent to the Roman DIANE, and the acronym stands for Automatic Retrieval of Text from Europe's Multinational Information Service. The name was proposed by the ADL project leader at a Euronet/DIANE user forum and has been adopted in this report as a convenient shorthand for a document digitalisation and teletrans-mission service for full text delivery.

DIANE is operational today. The acronym stands for Direct Information Access Network for Europe. It represents the ensemble of information services available through the Euronet tele-communications network. Euronet itself is a data transmission facility, not an information service.

DIANE provides a framework for the services that major European hosts offer via Euronet. The hosts are typically computer service bureaux which store bibliographic data bases. By providing a medium for the introduction of common features, such as standard command language, referral service and user guidance, DIANE presents a clearer image to the user of the wide range of information services available through the network.

ARTEMIS should build on the experience gained with DIANE, and supplement it. On-line search services, such as those available from DIANE, enable the user to identify promising references in the literature quickly and easily. But the user's needs are not satisfied until he has a copy of the full text of the relevant articles. ARTEMIS would be a speedy, comprehensive and economic document delivery service, accepting requests in the form of bibliographic references and fulfil-ling them by teletransmission from data bases of digitalised documents.

ARTEMIS would provide through a network of computers and communications links, a *conduit* via which an information provider can deliver the full text, or *content*, of a document to an information user on demand. (See Figure A.) The distinction between conduit and content is fundamental to the design and operation of information services. Communication between author and reader is achieved by deliverying a message – 'content' – through a medium – 'conduit'. Regulators of, and owners of rights in, content, such as censors or authors, seek to control access for social or economic reasons. Regulators and operators of conduits, such as the PTTs, aim for free flow of information with integrity and universality. The operators of conduits must provide a mechanism by which means those with interests in the content can achieve their legitimate aims. Otherwise, those with a stake in the content will establish their own conduits in order to control access to the information, or refuse to co-operate with the conduit provider.

The message that would pass through the medium of ARTEMIS from information provider to user is the document or 'full text'. This can be in the form of a facsimile of the original document (fax), or it can contain the author's text without preserving the layout or type font which we shall refer to as teletex or text. Recommendations for standards for both facsimile and teletex services are expected to be agreed at the 1980 Plenary Assembly of the CCITT.

ARTEMIS would be a store-and-forward system, which accepts information from a provider when it is available, and delivers it to a user when he wants it. Like a library, ARTEMIS would stock information in anticipation of need.

ARTEMIS should be an open system: any participant, whether information provider or user, would have the ability to communicate with any other, regardless of who owns or supplies the equipment involved. It would, therefore, operate like a marketplace in which buyers and sellers come together. Figure B shows the perspectives of providers and users.

The principle advantage of an open system is that additional subscribers enhance the value of the total system to existing subscribers. (The more people you can reach by telephone, the more valuable your telephone is to you.) ARTEMIS could have been conceived as a closed system, by means of which a fulfilment centre delivers documents to terminals located on the premises of users. Some stock market price display systems are of this kind. This would be inconsistent with the aim to create a broader market for information services.

The tangible components of ARTEMIS are shown in Figure C. There would be digitalisers and word processing terminals to create digital versions of documents. They may belong to libraries, publishers, businesses or other *information providers*. The information providers would arrange with the operators of computer systems to be *hosts* to the data bases of information. Some information providers may operate their own host computers, while other host computers would actively seek information providers to fill their data bases.

The host computers would be attached to a telecommunications network which links them to the terminals of the information *users*. The network itself would be provided by the PTTs. Initially, ARTEMIS should use Euronet, which is a PTT-operated data transmission network (co-financed with the CEC), which already links DIANE hosts to one single Community-wide facility. It is

FIGURE A

ARTEMIS
A CONDUIT FOR THE CONTENTS OF DOCUMENTS

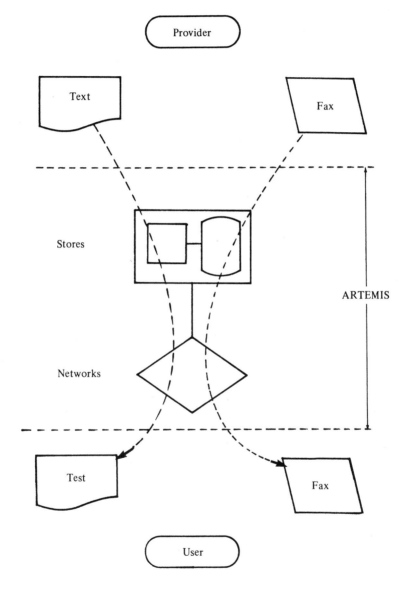

FIGURE B
TWO VIEWS OF ARTEMIS

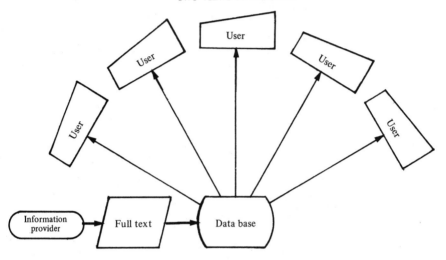

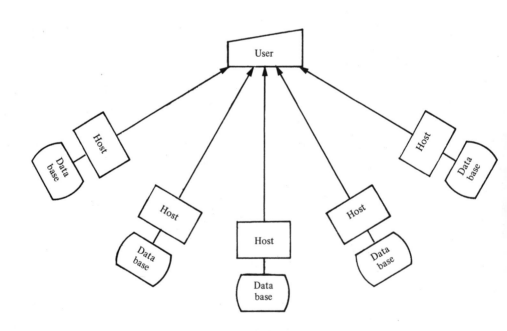

FIGURE C

TANGIBLE COMPONENTS OF ARTEMIS

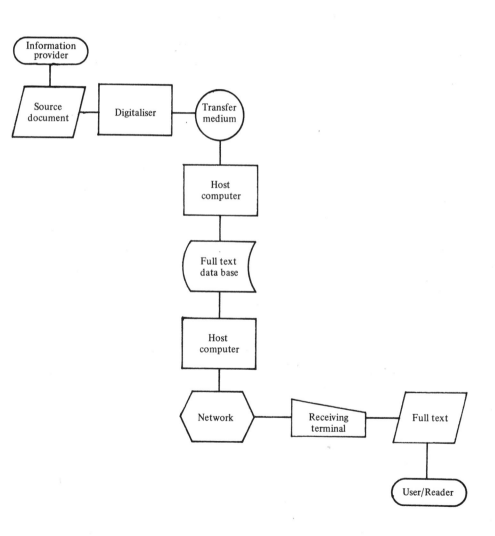

intended to give fast, cheap and reliable *remote access* to scientific, technical, social and economic information on-line. However, as the system grows, there may be links between ARTEMIS
participants which come to carry such high traffic densities that a leased line between them
would be jusified. There could also be circumstances under which distribution of full text by
satellite would be warranted.

ARTEMIS users would have terminals to which the host computers transmit documents. The
terminals would have to conform to facsimile or to teletex standards. Users of the former would
receive pages at the rate of about one per minute, and ARTEMIS would appear to them rather
like a distributed photocopier. Users of teletex terminals could think of ARTEMIS as a rather
superior telex, delivering text at the rate of several pages per minute.

The teletex and facsimile standards define *virtual terminals*. Many suppliers can provide real
terminals conforming to the standards, but it is also possible to program a computer so that it
appears to the network as if it were an actual terminal. Big ARTEMIS users could receive their
documents on such a computer, storing the bit-stream on a local file. They would then print the
documents on a high speed device.

Complementing the tangible components of ARTEMIS are the intangible contents of the data
bases. These would contain, either in facsimile or in teletex format, the documents stored by the
information providers. There would be a *prospective* collection of newly published material for
which a demand can be anticipated. There would be a *retrospective* collection of previously
published material, some of going back many years but known to be still in demand. Finally,
some material would be added *on demand*, the fulfilment centre treating ARTEMIS as a distributed copier which retains a copy for its own archives while delivering the user's request.

An ARTEMIS user would enter his order from a terminal, or by mail or telephone. Many of the
orders would originate from bibliographic searches using Euronet/DIANE, which should provide
correct bibliographic references. ARTEMIS would use the reference, which must be correct and
in standard format, to search the location index and discover which data base contained the
requested document. The order would cross the telecommunications network to the data base's
host computer which would find the document in its file.

The data base files might be on-line to the computer when the request arrived, or stored in a
media library from which they must be retrieved and mounted on the computer. Overnight, the
host computer would transmit the text across the network to the requestor's terminal. Generally, such terminals are capable of operating unattended and may either print the document as it
arrives, or store it on a local memory for printing under an operator's supervision in the morning.

The ARTEMIS accounting system would record the participants in each transaction: users, index
searcher, data base host and information provider. The user's payment would be divided in
accordance with agreements to be established between the other participants.

ADL concluded that ARTEMIS was technically feasible, but that market forces would not bring it into being. The scale of operation and extent of co-operation between parties with different interests are beyond what entrepreneurs or small co-operative ventures can achieve.

We therefore recommend to CEC DG XIII that it promote ARTEMIS by establishing a demonstration project. The first step would be a 'test bed' to prove the technology, establish interface standards, stimulate interests among equipment suppliers and hosts, and determine equipment costs and performance.

The second step would be a pilot project, using technology available today and proved on the 'test bed', which would awaken user and information provider interest, determine performance targets and operating costs, and hence establish pricing policy. It would also act as a catalyst for agreements on copyright protection and the linking of hosts and information providers.

In the third step, the single host and single data base used for the pilot project would be joined by others offering the same basic service to many more users. This open system would be characterised by common standards implemented in many different kinds of hardware.

DG XIII could now withdraw to the sidelines, leaving the market to encourage additional services, such as colour facsimile, on-line browsing and searching, demand and remote publishing, electronic journals and editorial offices, automatic translation and abstracting and so on.

To achieve this development, DG XIII will have to invite tenders and let contracts to provide *hardware, software* and *data base,* and to perform services such as digitalisation. It must also establish working groups, as was done with Euronet/DIANE, to define standards and procedures, and undertake the initial managerial and promotional work, including support to participants.

If DG XIII succeeds in lauching ARTEMIS, then it will have achieved:

●	Improved access to scientific and technical information in Europe by users in industry, commerce, the professions and academia;

●	A common market for information in Europe, which makes available the full range of material, not just national collections, to all users;

●	A marketplace and conduit through which information providers can serve information users;

●	The creation of an opportunity, not a threat, for existing stakeholders in the information business;

●	The encouragement of a variety of working arrangements among participants;

●	An allowance for national differences in the organisation of information provision and document delivery;

●	A vehicle for organisational experiments and test marketing of new information products and services;

7

- The exploitation of organisational advances in standardisation and harmonisation in Europe;

- The development of new standards and the promotion of existing ones;

- A worthwhile service at an acceptable price following the completion of a pilot project.

1. INTRODUCTION

1.1 The Reason for ADL's Study

In August 1979, ADL was commissioned by the Directorate General for Scientific and Technical Information and Information Management (DG XIII of the CEC), to conduct a study of: 'Document Digitalisation and Teletransmission'. ADL were to identify and analyse mechanisms:

- Enabling a transition to digital storage and transmission techniques;
- Required for the cost effective transmission of documents.

The 'Problems of Document Delivery for the Euronet User' were discussed in a technical report prepared for the CEC by the Franklin Institute last year. On-line search services for scientific and technical information (STI) enable the user to identify promising references in the literature quickly and easily. But the user's needs are not met until he has a full text copy of the relevant articles, so a speedy, comprehensive and economic document delivery service is needed. The planning study prepared by the Franklin consultants sheds light on the requirements, problems and possible solutions for document ordering and delivery on Euronet/DIANE.

The EEC Committee for Information and Documentation in Science and Technology (CIDST) considered the report and the comments and recommendations of others who studied it, and recommended additional technical studies.

ADL has undertaken two of these, looking at the closely related technological, economic and managerial issues of converting documents to digital form and delivering them by teletransmission. The background to the study is the rapid development of computing and telecommunications technology which might already, or could be expected in the near future to, provide the means of electronic document delivery. This could eliminate, or cut down significantly, the movement of paper currently supplied by a document fulfilment centre to a reader.

ADL has not studied the important issues of copyright and document ordering. Nor has it investigated the possible improvements that might be made to today's methods of delivery, since it was asked to determine the feasibility of *new methods*. We start from the point at which a fulfilment centre receives a correct request for a document that it is authorised to deliver to the reader.

9

1.2   Study Methodology

ADL began by looking at many ideas and concepts for a document delivery service mentioned in the literature, discussed at conferences or suggested to us during discussions. We focussed on those solutions to the document delivery problem which required digitalisation and teletransmission.

We then looked at the state-of-the-art in all the critical technologies: digitalisation of documents by optical character recognition (OCR) and facsimile scanning; word and text processing and photocomposition; digital communications by terrestrial and satellite networks; storage media for digitalised documents; computer hardware and software; terminals and printers. We concluded that the necessary technology for each part of a document delivery system already exists, and future developments will reduce costs and improve performance.

We also looked at the nature of the documents containing scientific and technical information, which would have to be digitalised and stored. We realised that for some years, the delivery system would handle only a small sub-set of a vast universe of documents, so there is no immediate call for a system with a capacity to store most of the stock of scientific and technical information.

We reported our interim conclusions and received valuable comments on how to solve the primary problem: assembling the individual components, whose technical feasibility had been established, into an overall system which could provide a document delivery service.

We developed various scenarios, and selected the most likely as the basis for this report. We have distilled the results of our researches into this comparatively brief report, discarding deliberately many interesting ideas that we explored but rejected during our study. However, a few points from some of these have been written up and included here too.

1.3   Conclusions

1.3.1   Summary of Conclusions

ADL's study shows that ARTEMIS is technically feasible. We believe that market forces will not bring such a system about. If the demand for quick access to full texts is to be satisfied, then a demonstration project is required.

ARTEMIS must develop as an open system, through which any information provider can deliver documents to any user. It must therefore be based on international standards.

Further technical studies are needed to determine how to apply existing technology to ARTEMIS.

Important non-technical issues must be resolved before ARTEMIS can flourish.

1.3.2   ARTEMIS is Technically Feasible

The components of ARTEMIS are available today among the products offered by the computing and communications industry. These components are:

- Digital facsimile scanners;
- Text and word processors;
- Optical character readers;
- Communication networks for digital data;
- Digital computers with network interfaces;
- Digital storage devices attached to computers;
- Text printers and composers;
- Facsimile receivers.

The software to bring these components together into a system is well within the state-of-the-art.

1.3.3   Market Forces Alone Will Not Bring About Such A System

ADL did not undertake market research, but the impression gained from discussions with many potential participants in ARTEMIS was that no individual enterprise, nor small consortium, could launch ARTEMIS. Too much co-operation from traditional competitors, and too many legal and regulatory accommodations, are required for entrepreneurs to risk initiating the project. However, we gained the further impression that many might join in the development of ARTEMIS.

11

1.3.4   A Demonstration Project Is Required

Although the components of ARTEMIS are available, the complete system has never been assembled. So a 'test bed' to demonstrate technical feasibility is essential. This will establish the standards for interfacing components to each other and test the software that controls the movement of information from document to store, and from store to printer.

The 'test bed' can develop into a pilot project, needed to determine the operating economics of ARTEMIS and to test the market.

1.3.5   ARTEMIS Should Be An Open System

Any information provider, host computer operator or information user who joins ARTEMIS enhances its value to the others and to the communications carriers. Only the hosts need fear competition from each other, but not till the market approaches saturation far in the future. So an open system is appropriate, rather than a closed one in which the managing group determines what information may be provided and who may subscribe to the service. (There is no reason why ARTEMIS should not contain closed user groups within an open system.)

International standards make joining ARTEMIS much easier, because potential participants may have the necessary equipment already, or will find a wider range offered on the market.

1.3.6   Further Technical Studies Must Be Undertaken

Although we have concluded that all the hardware components are now available, many practical problems must be solved effectively and economically. Examples include:

- The interfacing of Group 3 facsimile receivers to Euronet;

- The loading of data bases from facsimile scanners;

- The development of procedures and software for:

    - Locating documents;
    - Accounting;
    - Ordering;

- The connection of non-standard terminals via 'black boxes'.

1.3.7   Agreement Must Be Reached On Non-Technical Issues

Many non-technical issues remain to be resolved before ARTEMIS can grow to its full potential. ADL did not study many of the most important of these, such as copyright, and cannot venture any conclusion about the resolution of the conflicting interests. However, it is believed that the overall benefits of ARTEMIS are sufficient to ensure that all participants can gain.

1.4   Structure of the Report

The management summary is an integral part of this report. In subsequent sections, we describe the document delivery problem and technical solutions: i.e. what needs to be done and what can be done.

We then look at non-technical issues which determine the acceptability and practicability of the possible technical approaches.

We expect our readers to include many who do not have technical knowledge or familiarity with the language of the information industry. Rather than breaking the flow of narrative with explanations of terms, we have appended a glossary.

All costs and prices are in European Currency Units, (ECUs). Where appropriate, we have shown the original currency as well. A conversion table is included in the glossary under 'ECU'.

2.   THE DOCUMENT DELIVERY PROBLEM

2.1   Today's Methods of Document Delivery

A document delivery service must place the author's thoughts, in text or graphic form, in front of the reader.

Figure 2.1.A shows, in a simplified schematic diagram, how a final document is built up in a six stage production process. Each stage adds information which can be captured in different variants of the journal. At one extreme, the electronic journal may not even be edited; at the other, the reader gets the benefit of the marginal notes of a previous reader.

ARTEMIS will pick up the editor's output, either by character recognition or, during text editing, as a by-product; or it will take the compositor's output by facsimile. Eventually, some production processes, including authorship and editing, will be changed to exploit ARTEMIS.

However, today the user must order a document from a fulfilment centre, such as a library, and will receive the printed version, a photocopy or a microform by mail or messenger. Thus the author's material is conveyed on a medium requiring physical transport to the user.

On-line searches, such as those made possible by Euronet/DIANE, will not only increase demand for documents, but create user frustration as a result of slow delivery. Orders have to be sent in, processed at the fulfilment centre, and sent out by mail or messenger service. Improvements in all these stages are needed, and as each gets better, delay in others will become relatively more significant.

Given a satisfactory ordering procedure, a correct citation can be provided to a document fulfilment centre. (It was not part of ADL's study to consider the ordering process, nor the mechanism for determining which of the possibly many fulfilment centres should meet a user request.) However, solving the ordering problem does not solve the delivery problem.

A reader who orders a document has a limited reading capacity, and will not require large quantities of material to be delivered within seconds. However, he may want a small quantity within a few minutes and substantial volumes of material within a day or two.

Today, it is quite likely he would have to wait for several days while the required document was found, and as much as a week or two for its delivery. Fulfilment of a request within a week is often regarded as satisfactory by the delivery service, and for much academic and industrial research, satisfies the user as well. But there remains a significant demand for a more rapid service which is capable of delivering a few pages within minutes and substantial sets of documents overnight.

FIGURE 2.1.A

DOCUMENT CREATION

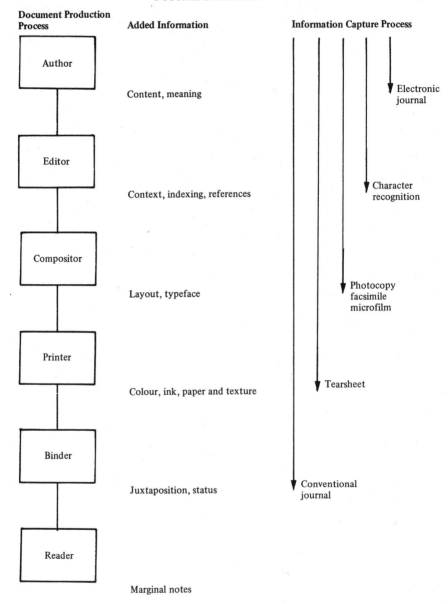

Document Production Process

Author

Editor

Compositor

Printer

Binder

Reader

Added Information

Content, meaning

Context, indexing, references

Layout, typeface

Colour, ink, paper and texture

Juxtaposition, status

Marginal notes

Information Capture Process

Electronic journal

Character recognition

Photocopy facsimile microfilm

Tearsheet

Conventional journal

2.2   Experiments to Improve Document Delivery

Each link in the chain from author to reader, alone or in combination, has been the subject of studies and experiments, some leading to operational services, to shorten the delivery time.

For example, the British Library in some areas uses a van service for deliveries which is often both cheaper and quicker than the mail. The Library of Congress in Washington DC undertook a 'Design Study of Text Access Facilities' to deliver the full text of cited documents to readers on Capitol Hill by retrieving them from a microfilm file and displaying them at a TV-type terminal.

The US National Science Foundation published a study* of no less than 88 innovations pertinent to publishing and information dissemination. Many of them reflect the advantages of digital computers and communications over the creation and physical movement of paper for information delivery. However, even such radical proposals as John Sender's 'On-line Scientific Journal'** will take their places alongside, while not replacing entirely, the paper-based publications, of which many already exist as conventional documents.

*PB 247–057 'Improving the Dissemination of Scientific and Technical Information: A Practitioner's
Guide to Innovation' by Capital Systems Group Inc. 1975
**Information Scientist, Volume 11, Number 1, March 1977, Pages 2–3

2.3 Requirements and Behaviour of Users of Scientific and Technical Information

2.3.1 Delivery Delay

The user's willingness to pay for quicker delivery or sacrifice higher quality for speed of delivery is shown conceptually in Figures 2.3.1.A and 2.3.1.B. In theory, both curves are concave to the origin, monotonic but stepped rather than smooth (e.g. the curve levels off from, say, 18.00 on one day till 08.00 the next).

These curves describe particular users on particular occasions. For a large number of users on different occasions, similar curves can be drawn to indicate the tolerable delay for a given proportion of the times for a given proportion of users (e.g. half the users, 90 per cent of the time). Users may prefer a predictable, but slower, delivery service to one that is usually faster, but cannot be relied upon. They also have quite different requirements for the documents and these can be classified as follows:

- Specific information;
- News;
- General information to maintain professional awareness.

Besides knowing the theoretical shape of these curves, there are also some practical measures related to documents in the two more urgent of these three requirement classes:

- Delivery quicker than reading speed (one page in one minute) is rarely useful to the reader himself, so the curve levels out below one minute*;

- Some works of reference lose almost all their value when the next edition is published, at which time the curve drops sharply;

- Where numerous documents are requested at the same time, overnight delivery is acceptable.

ARTEMIS may be able to offer three speeds of response:

FAST   Within minutes to the designated printer.

OVERNIGHT   Overnight to user's mailbox or printer.

WHEN FOUND   Search time for source document to be found and digitalised, then either FAST or OVERNIGHT delivery.

---

*Quicker delivery may be valuable for reasons other than the reader's ability to assimilate the content, such as: lower telecommunications charges or large volumes to be delivered in limited time.

18

FIGURE 2.3.1.A
USER'S WILLINGNESS TO PAY FOR QUICKER DELIVERY

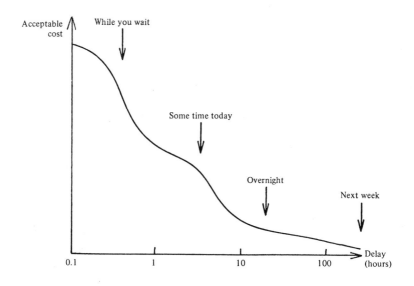

FIGURE 2.3.1.B
USER'S TOLERANCE OF LOWER QUALITY IN EXCHANGE FOR QUICKER DELIVERY

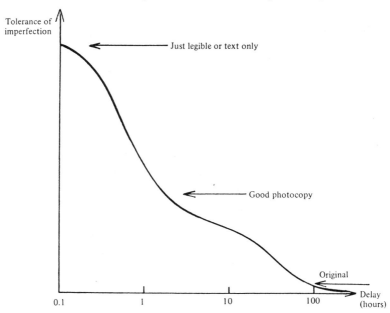

Computer service bureaux have demonstrated that for some data, some users will pay a premium for fast service. Quick delivery from printer to reader is essential if quick delivery from store to printer is to be worthwhile. This may limit the market for the FAST service to a few well-equipped user communities.

2.3.2 Document Quality

Eventually, ARTEMIS may become the sole means of publishing some documents. Until then, however, readers will measure the quality of a document by its faithfulness to the original. With a journal article, the published version from the printer defines the quality standard, and a photocopy would be a more or less acceptable substitute.

Information content is what the reader is generally seeking when he demands a 'good quality' copy. In practice, there will be different measures of quality for facsimile and teletex data in ARTEMIS. In the former, resolution will be the key parameter and we can expect the readers and ARTEMIS centres to determine through the marketplace how quality and price are related. Delay and quality will also be traded-off; sometimes the user will seek a 'quick-and-dirty' copy at his desk on a cheap facsimile receiver, at other times he will wait for a perfect copy to come from a better equipped print shop.

For teletex data, there will be another set of quality criteria, and a similar delay/quality trade-off. In larger organisations the reader may have some control over the printing process, perhaps being able to choose between a word processor in his office, a line or page printer in the computer room or a phototypesetter in his print shop. In smaller organisations, the reader may have access commercially to a similar choice of facilities, or might press his videotex system into service in an emergency. Whatever the size of the user and his print facilities, the originator of the document will not be able to specify type font, line length or page size.

We would expect market forces to lead to a range of services with various combinations of price, delay and document quality. Some readers may not have access at any price to high quality, high speed services since these are likely to be available only at metropolitan bureaux, on campuses and in large corporations.

2.4   Numbers and Types of Documents

To evaluate ARTEMIS completely, one would need to know the following:

● How much information must be digitalised:

- Continually, to keep up with new material;
- Initially, to load the backlog of previous publications of interest;

● How much information must be stored to meet requests;

● How much information must be delivered in response to requests.

Although ADL attempted to provide answers to all these questions, there are so many uncertainties that no forecast can be relied upon. The principal doubts centre on:

● The boundaries of the subject area designated Scientific and Technical Information;

● The proportion of relevant European and foreign information that would be digitalised, given:

- Copyright agreements or restrictions;
- Level of user interest;

● The amount of material other than journals and monographs to be added;

● The extent of the retrospective collection;

● The marketing and promotional effort put into ARTEMIS.

Despite these limitations, we did develop figures which were useful for assessing the economics of ARTEMIS. We needed to measure volume of data initially in pages, although most other researchers have counted titles. Our conversion factors are given in Table 2.4.A.

ARTEMIS will begin by storing documents that are, or can be expected to be, requested from it. Eventually, it will acquire routinely *all* documents within its area of interest (which may be constrained by, for example, copyright agreements) as they are published. This we refer to as the flow of material into ARTEMIS. The corresponding outflow is the fulfilled request rate which should be at least an order of magnitude higher than the inflow. Once a document has been acquired by ARTEMIS, it is never discarded; however, it may be relegated to an archival store from which retrieval may be slow and/or expensive. The accumulated inflow constitutes the 'stock' of literature available from ARTEMIS.

In assessing the volume of data to be stored, we included with the output of the nine EEC members some part of the foreign material. STI literature is international; e.g. subscriptions to US journals from abroad were 55 per cent in 1965 and 45 per cent in 1975. We expect ARTEMIS

21

TABLE 2.4.A

CONVERSION FACTORS FOR DATA VOLUMES

Number of pages in a book		340
Number of characters in a book		820,000
Number of characters on a page of a book		2,400

Journal issues per year		6.6
Journal pages per year		980

Pages of journal containing:	Articles (per annum)	740
	Advertising	60
	Other	180

Pages of text per article	4.7
Number of words per journal per year	280,000
Number of characters per page of journal	2,000
Number of articles per journal per year	160
Non-journal pages per year	850

All figures are rounded averages, derived from

(1) Resnikoff and Dolby, ACCESS, 1971
(2) King, **Worldwide Indicators**, 1977

to store as much foreign material as European unless prevented from so doing by legal or competitive moves. It is believed that the greater proportion of possible foreign literature stored in ARTEMIS will be journals rather than monographs, but there is no way of estimating either proportion.

The total numbers of titles were analysed by country, subject area, and type of material in the EEC and USA. The grand total for the EEC countries is almost two million, containing 40 million pages. If a great deal of foreign material were to be acquired by ARTEMIS, it might be necessary to store more than twice as much information as would have come from European sources alone.

ADL's best guesses at the annual total of titles and pages that might be added to ARTEMIS each year is shown in Table 2.4.B. It comes to about four million items containing 75 million pages.

ADL's own studies for the US National Periodicals Center bear out other reports of rapidly declining interest in books and journals with age. In general, five years of periodicals will satisfy about 80 per cent of requests. (Major fulfilment centres will have more requests for older material, since newer material is available from local or in-house sources.)

ARTEMIS will accumulate new material from its inception, and will also bring into store any other material that might be requested. An estimate of the amount of old material which will not be asked for at all, and which therefore will never enter the system, has not been calculated. However, the retrospective collection could be limited to, say, the most popular 20 per cent of material between five and ten years old, and ten per cent of that between ten and twenty years old, while still responding to almost all requests. It is believed that the total stock in ARTEMIS will grow as shown in Figure 2.4.C. By the mid 1980s ARTEMIS could have in stock about ten years output at 1980 rates and might be growing at 20 per cent per annum as it gathers in the backlog.

The number of requests for documents to be delivered by ARTEMIS depends critically on the cost, performance and comprehensiveness of the system. Before it has reached maturity, the rate of penetration and the level of marketing effort will also have significant effects on demand.

The Franklin report estimated the following:

Total European searches - 1978	200,000
Total number of hits per search	85
Total relevant hits	30
Total number of document requests for STI in EEC - 1978	6,000,000

TABLE 2.4.B

**ESTIMATED NUMBER OF TITLES AND PAGES
TO BE STORED IN ARTEMIS EACH YEAR**

	Titles thousands	Pages millions
Periodical articles	1,400.0	6.7
Books	35.5	12.1
Pamphlets[1]	6.2	0.3
Corporate reports	0.9	0.05
Patents	250.0	12.4
Technical reports	143.0	
Proceedings	9.0	8.5[2]
Dissertations	17.0	
EEC TOTAL (rounded)	**1,860.0**	**40.0**
FOREIGN TOTAL	**2,240.0**	**35.0**
GRAND TOTAL	**4,100.0**	**75.0**

(1) For definition, see glossary
(2) ADL estimate of 50 pages each

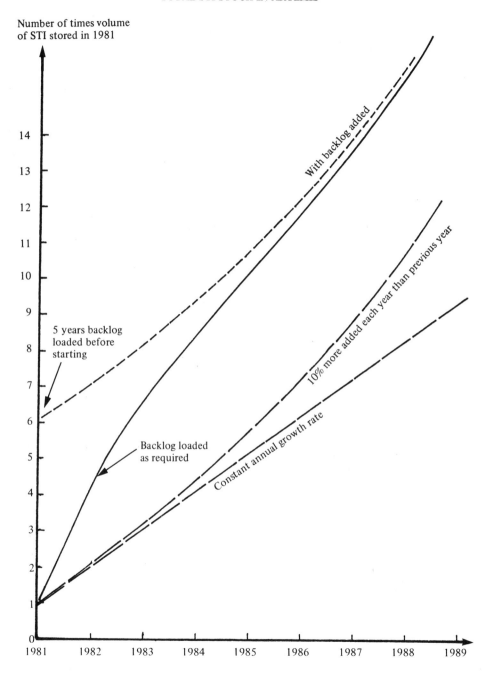

FIGURE 2.4.C

TOTAL STI STOCK IN ARTEMIS

Number of times volume
of STI stored in 1981

With backlog added

5 years backlog
loaded before
starting

10% more added each year than previous year

Backlog loaded
as required

Constant annual growth rate

14

13

12

11

10

9

8

7

6

5

4

3

2

1

0

1981 1982 1983 1984 1985 1986 1987 1988 1989

25

The authors were forced to make some heroic assumptions about the impact of on-line searching and the ability of in-house services to fulfill requests before reaching the conclusion that ten million requests might be made in 1981 for external delivery.

If ARTEMIS were to become a substitute for in-house subscriptions to journals, then the request rate for fulfilment might well to rise.

For the analyses of costs and benefits the figure of ten million document fulfilment requests per annum to ARTEMIS at maturity has been used.

Competition from other sources, restrictions on ARTEMIS's scope, or slow growth could reduce this to one million per annum at maturity. Conversely, successful promotion, high performance and low prices might raise demand from ten million to 100 million per annum, in which case ARTEMIS would be the dominant source of STI in Europe.

2.5   Present Delivery Costs

The cost to the end user of document delivery depends on many variables, some of which he does not recognise explicitly. The fulfilment centre may include all costs in an overall charge, or itemise and pass on some of them, such as postage.

One fulfilment centre, the British National Computing Centre, has a simple price schedule and charges 0.30 ECU (20 pence) per page, inclusive of mail costs, and irrespective of order size. By contrast, the US DIALOGUE DIALORDER^{TM} service has a complex schedule, as shown in Table 2.5.A. Table 2.5.B shows that copying accounts for about one quarter of the page charge from DIALORDER.

A fulfilment centre's costs include:

- Equipment;
- Operator time (including finding the document);
- Materials;
- Transport;

and these vary with:

- Number and size of pages and number of documents in an order;
- Equipment utilisaton;
- Contribution of user (e.g. paper on a fax receiver).

Mail charges are often as high as 10 to 20 cents US (0.06 to 0.12 ECUs) per page since a typical fulfilment package may have only a few pages.

The user seldom recognises the internal cost of delivery from his mail room to his desk; however, this cost will not vary much between delivery methods unless he has a desk top terminal.

Fulfilment of document requests by mail costs the user on average between 0.30 and 0.60 ECUs per page, of which 0.15 ECUs is passed on to the mail carrier by the fulfilment centre.

TABLE 2.5.A

US DIALOG DIALORDER[TM] SERVICE
EXTRACTS FROM PRICE SCHEDULE, December 1979

	US Dollars	ECU
Minimum billing	20.00	14.00
Per item charge	5.00–8.00	3.50–5.60
Per page charge	0.25	0.17
Telefax charge	at cost	–
Postage and delivery	at cost	–
Copyright fee	~ 4.50 usually	3.15

TABLE 2.5.B

COST OF COPYING
US cents per copy, 1975

Cost components	Type of Copy		
	Plain paper	Coated paper	Thermal
Paper	0.3–0.4	3.0	6.3
Toner	0.25	0.1	–
Machine usage	3.4	1.5	0.4
Total	4.0	4.6	6.7
Total (in ECU's x 100)	2.8	3.3	4.7
Annual production (milliard copies)	60	14	3
% rented machines	95	25–30	small

From an ADL study, 1975

28

3. TECHNICAL SOLUTIONS TO THE DELIVERY PROBLEM

3.1 Telecommunications Development

The telecommunications developments make ARTEMIS technically and economically feasible in the 1980s. Because no physical movement of paper is needed to convey information from author to reader, the speed of delivery is determined by the movement of electronic signals, not vehicular transport or human messengers.

Computer networks like Euronet/DIANE, which were created during the 1970s, reflect two significant advances: technological progress in electronics and transmission media; and a deeper understanding of how networks function, reflected in improved network architecture.

ARTEMIS can be thought of as an *architecture*, which, when *implemented* by the participants, results in a *system* to provide a *service* to users.

The precise definition of the functions that ARTEMIS and its components should perform is its *architecture*. How these functions are performed using software, hardware and people, is the *implementation*, which should conform to the architecture. Different network architectures have been put forward by computer manufacturers (e.g. IBM's Systems Network Architecture) and telecommunications common carriers (e.g. Transpac). However, all of them involve a layered structure with *protocols* for communication between pairs of layers at the same peer-level (see Figure 4.5.A below).

ISO, recognising the problems of incompatible architectures, has proposed a 'Provisional Architectural Model'* on which ARTEMIS should be based. It contains seven functional or control levels:

1. Physical control   ⎫
2. Link control   ⎬ Transport service
3. Network control   ⎪
4. Transport end-to-end control ⎭
5. Session control
6. Presentation control
7. Application

Standards already exist for levels one to three, but not for the other four. Levels one through four provide a *transport service* to layer five, the session control. This layer sets up, maintains and terminates logical connections between an ARTEMIS host and a user terminal so that the user's request can pass between them.

*'Reference Model of Open Systems Architecture' ISO/TC97/XC16/N117 (November 1978)

29

Layer six, presentation control, provides data formats and transforms data, for example, by compressing and encyphering them, or expanding and decoding them to print out on a facsimile receiver.

The top layer, number seven, is the application or end user. In ARTEMIS, this would be a program within a host computer which retrieves the requested text, at one end, and the person (or a program in his intelligent terminal) calling for the text to be delivered at the other end.

ARTEMIS would exploit the technological developments used in the implementation of the transport service. A public data network (PDN) will link users and host initially, and later might be supplemented, or partially substituted, by leased terrestrial circuits or satellite transponders, if the volumes and economics warranted it.

ARTEMIS is conceived as an open system providing a *conduit* through which the *content* of any information provider's data base can be delivered to any user. By basing ARTEMIS on a PDN, any user has access to the conduit.

The first PDNs were introduced in Canada and France about ten years ago, using analogue transmission and modems. Meanwhile, digital techniques were being applied in the telephone network and the USA, Brazil and Japan followed Canada in exploiting these for data communications over leased circuits. Now, fast circuit switched digital services are available or planned by several European countries.

During the 1960s, the concept of packet switching was developed and demonstrated, and public networks were implemented in the 1970s. For ARTEMIS, the most important of these is Euronet. The CCITT has produced recommendations regarding services to be provided by PDNs based on packet switching, and Euronet conforms to these. It follows that any user terminal attached to Euronet would be able to send requests and receive back documents.

However, the use of Euronet initially need not preclude the use of other networks in future. Where large volumes of data are to be exchanged between ARTEMIS hosts, or between hosts and large printing centres, leased lines may be cheaper. Furthermore, some hosts may already have such lines for applications other than ARTEMIS.

There are promising developments in satellite communications which might ultimately provide very cheap delivery of documents to small rooftop antennae. The European Space Agency's work should be followed closely with a view to incorporating satellite communications among the ways of linking hosts and users. The PTTs may provide such a service themselves, encourage experiments, or licence a trial service. However, the launching of ARTEMIS is not dependent on the development of any such new technology.

Even the most optimistic projections of ARTEMIS's growth do not suggest that its data volumes will have a significant impact on PTT revenues, or require more than a fraction of the capacity of a communications satellite. However, the overnight delivery requirement of documents means that ARTEMIS would use communications links which will otherwise be idle. The PTTs may therefore be willing to negotiate favourable tariffs for Euronet/ARTEMIS.

PTT tariffs may be based on:

- Distance;
- Duration of connection;
- Time of day;
- Data volume;
- Link speed;
- Minimum charges;
- Volume discounts;
- Connection charges;
- National borders.

It is therefore a complex exercise to calculate the optimal network configuration, particularly when many users will require the same facilities for applications other than ARTEMIS. Furthermore, some of the charges may be determined by negotiation, not by published tariff. Indeed, the tariffs themselves are being reviewed and may be reduced for all file-to-file data transfers, of which ARTEMIS would be only one example. Once again, ARTEMIS is not dependent on lower tariffs to be viable, although it would benefit significantly from any reduction.

In the cost calculations, it is assumed that Euronet would be used at present overnight rates. Table 3.1.A gives the tariff and two examples of page transmission costs.

TABLE 3.1.A

EURONET TARIFF, UK, CHEAP RATE

(UK Sterling)

		Leased lines	Dial up
Once only charges		£150.00	£25
Annual rental	— 1,200 bps	£143.75	£20
	— 9,600 bps	£200.00	
Duration charge	— 1,200 bps	1.4 p per min.	1.8 p per min.
	— 9,600 bps	1.8 p per min.	
Volume charge	— per 10,000 bits	1.56p	1.56p
	— per 10 data segments	0.8 p	0.8 p

Examples

1. Large user of leased line at 9,600 bps, requesting ten pages of facsimile (2.10^6 bits), 10,000 times per year:

			Cost per page	
			Pence	ECU
Annual cost per page	$\dfrac{£200 + £150 \times 20\%*}{100,000}$	=	0.23	.035
Duration cost at 20 seconds per page		=	0.6	.092
Volume cost (at 98% packing of segments)		=	31.8	.489
TOTAL			**32.6**	**.616**

2. Small user dialling in at 1,200 bps, requesting ten pages of teletex 100 times per year:

			Cost per page	
			Pence	ECU
Annual cost per page	$\dfrac{£20 + £25 \times 20\%*}{1,000}$	=	2.5	.038
Duration cost at 18 seconds per page		=	0.5	.008
Phone call charge at 3p minimum for 12 minutes		=	0.6	.009
Volume cost (at 80% packing of segments)		=	3.1	.048
TOTAL			**6.7**	**.103**

*Amortisation of once only charge over five years

32

3.2   Storage Developments

No new technology would be required to store full texts in ARTEMIS's data bases, but current developments promise even lower costs and higher speeds during the next decade.

An ARTEMIS archive would contain strings of bits created by digitalising pages of documents. Typical pages will contain about 10^4 bits or 2.10^5 bits for teletex and facsimile versions respectively. (See Section 3.3 below.) So a data base containing ten million pages, or a million journal articles, must store of the order of 10^{11} to 10^{12} bits. Some computers will be hosts to much smaller data bases, others could be a hundred times larger.

All suitable storage devices in the range 10^9 to 10^{15} bits are classified in data processing usage as archival. These will form part of the hierarchy of storage media, the fastest and smallest of which uses fast *semiconductor* or *magnetic bubble* media for the temporary storage of about 10^7 bits. Data from the slower, larger archives will be read very rapidly into the fast memory, and then passed through the computer onto the telecommunications lines which typically accept data 10^3 to 10^4 times more slowly than it can be read from the archives.

Some storage hierarchies will include *moving head disks* with capacities of about 10^9 to 10^{10} bits and access times to any information at random of 25 milliseconds or less. Such media are suitable for browsing and on-line searching and are generally used by the DIANE hosts for their bibliographic data bases. Some hosts may make part of their full text archives available in this readily accessible form; topical material, law reports and safety information are candidates.

However, the vast majority of requests for full texts can be met by overnight access and delivery. A collection of thousands of documents would be stored on a demountable module, which normally sits on a rack in a 'media library'. On any one night only a small sub-set of modules will be loaded by the operator, since no requests would have come for documents on the majority of modules in the collection. In any module mounted, very few of the thousands of pages will be wanted, so the computer needs to search and find the right ones in a minute or so. (If it takes much longer, the number of drives required to complete all the searches in the night hours becomes unacceptably high.)

Mass storage systems are based on magnetic tape, magnetic cartridge or video tape. (See Table 3.2.A and Figure 3.2.A.) They already have capacities of 10^{10} to 10^{12} bits on-line at any time and will increase in capacity and drop in price 100-fold during the next decade (see Figure 3.2.B).

Optical mass storage and *optical video disk* have the advantage of being 'read-only',* but are still being developed. Their capacities and costs will improve more rapidly than mass storage and might well be preferred by ARTEMIS hosts in the mid 1980s.

---

*Archival stores of the ARTEMIS kind would be written only once and read many times unlike conventional data processing systems in which updating of stored data is frequently required. When the medium is **magnetic**, erasure and rewriting are possible, whereas **optical** media are read-only following the initial writing.

TABLE 3.2.A

CAPACITY AND COST VS. TIME

Memory technology	Typical capacity	Access time	Cost
Magnetic cartridge, video and tape mass storage systems	1.1 terabits[1]	7 to 15 seconds	29 to 190 microcents per bit
Optical mass storage	1.0 terabits	7 to 20 seconds	360 microcents per bit
Optical video disk	0.01 terabits[2]	7.5 seconds (future — less than one second)	Up to 20 microcents per bit[2]
Holographic memories	0.2 terabits[2]	Less than 15 seconds (future in millisecond range)	2.5 microcents per bit for the media[2]

(1) 1 terabit = 10^{12} bits. (See Glossary.)
(2) Estimates of current devices

FIGURE 3.2.A

CAPACITY VS. TIME

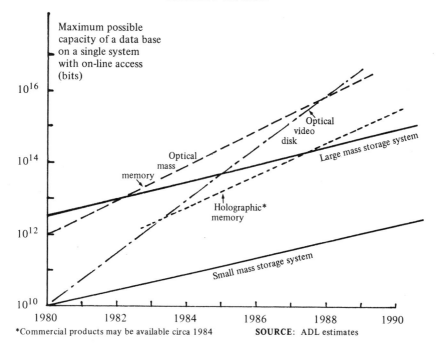

Maximum possible
capacity of a data base
on a single system
with on-line access
(bits)

*Commercial products may be available circa 1984　　　　SOURCE: ADL estimates

FIGURE 3.2.B

COST VS. TIME

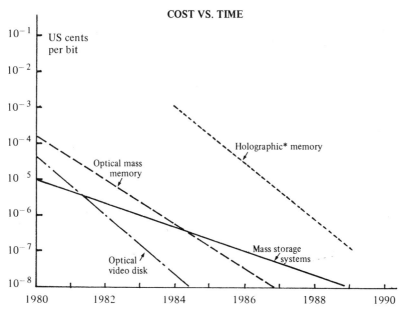

*Commercial products may be available circa 1984

Holographic memories are still experimental, but some forecasters expect them to be the cheapest medium by the end of the decade.

A typical-five page journal article, stored as text, contains about 5×10^4 bits and costs about 0.01 to 0.07 ECUs to store today. The facsimile version would cost 0.12 to 1.20 ECU on a mass storage device, and will be ten times cheaper by the mid 1980s.

3.3 The Data Content of a Page

ARTEMIS would handle two distinct versions of documents: one coded for delivery by teletex, the other coded for facsimile transmission.

The number of characters on a journal page delivered by teletex is about 2,000 (a book page has about 2,400). Using the standard eight-bit alphabet (ISO 4873:1979), this produces 16,000 bits. However, simple coding to eliminate redundancy can cut this number by a factor of two to five, whilst a seven-bit code (ISO 646:1973) also reduces the number of bits. In this report, 10,000 bits (10^4) per page of text has been assumed when estimating storage requirements, 16,000 for transmission by teletex.

The calculation for Group 3 facsimile representation is more complex. An A4 page has an area of about 600 square centimetres and is scanned at eight lines per millimetre horizontally and 2.5, 3.8 or 7.7 lines per millimetre vertically depending on resolution. At standard resolution, there are almost 2×10^6 bits per page. According to CCITT standards, this data string is compressed (using Modified Huffman Coding, MHC) and will take less than one minute to transmit at 4,800 bits per second, a six-fold compression to 3.10^5 bits.

Still higher compression is possible and CCITT is looking at no less than seven proposals, which all have similar performance with respect to compression, susceptibility to transmission errors, complexity of implementation and compatibility with MHC. Twenty-fold compression may be possible, so a high resolution page with 3.8×10^6 bits can be stored as 2.10^5 bits. (See Table 3.3.A.)

TABLE 3.3.A

DATA CONTENT OF A TYPICAL A4 FACSIMILE PAGE

Resolution		Transmission (MHC version, 4800 bps)		Storage (With further compression)
Lines per mm	Bits	Bits	Seconds	Bits
2.5	1.3×10^6	2×10^5	40	7×10^4
3.8	2.0×10^6	3×10^5	60	1×10^5
7.7	3.8×10^6	6×10^5	120	2×10^5

In this report it is assumed that all *transmission* will use MHC at standard resolution, so an A4 page would contain 3.10^5 bits. This is because normal users will want to use standard machines and pay for adequate resolution only. Since many technical journals use a smaller page than A4, the average page transmitted will contain about 2.10^5 bits.

However, the documents may be *stored* at high resolution and high compression, which requires 2.10^5 bits for an A4 page. Stores will wish to meet requests for the higher resolution, and can afford the extra processing to compress and expand; they do not need to be compatible with any user, provided they can recreate the uncompressed image.

Documents vary in content widely, some containing a lot of white space, others an information-packed image. So our average figure of 2.10^5 bits per page could vary from collection to collection by a factor of two. Furthermore, some stores may expand small type fonts, such as those in newspaper articles, or reduce large ones before storing, changing the effective resolution delivered to the reader and the bits stored per input page.

3.4 Document Capture

A facsimile image of a document can be captured from paper or microfilm. Information providers, such as publishers or fulfilment centres, with large collections to digitalise might install machines which are faster than conventional facsimile transmitters with better paper or microfilm handling equipment, and capable of scanning and transmitting one page per second to a computer. Such equipment is still experimental, but is under development for operation with the Satellite Business Systems* project. It should be available in time for the major growth of ARTEMIS following the pilot project. A digitalising facility handling ten million pages per annum with a full time operator should be feasible at a cost of 60,000 ECUs per anumm or less, which is less than 0.01 ECUs per page.

A conventional Group 3 facsimile transmitter can be fitted with a hopper to read single sheets and be left to read them directly onto a transmission line connected to an ARTEMIS host computer at the rate of one every two minutes. Such a transmitter can load 50,000 pages per annum at an annual cost of 5,000 ECUs or 0.10 ECUs per page, including labour costs of ten per cent of an operator's time.

ADL recommends that tenders be invited to supply two such systems, one to handle microfiche and microfilm, the other to handle loose sheets, for delivery in 1983. In addition, about ten systems to handle one million pages per annum each may be needed the following year for installation at the major fulfilment centres in Europe. The very fast system would be devoted to a planned loading of the retrospective collection and new material in anticipation of demand. The other machines would fulfill requests for hitherto undigitalised material by adding material from paper or microform collections to the ARTEMIS data base for onward transmission.

A text suitable for teletex transmission can be captured either by optical character recognition from existing paper or microfilm documents, or by taking the record of keystrokes on a machine-readable medium created during text processing. (In principle, it would be possible to copy-type documents into the data base, but the cost would be high.)

OCR may be suitable for capturing a small sub-set of existing material with a limited type font and no significant images. A special facility costing a few million ECUs could read five million pages per annum; a slower system costing 60,000 ECUs can handle one page per minute or two hundred thousand per annum. So each page, in either case, would cost about 0.30 ECUs. (A copy typist would cost about 0.60 ECUs per page.)

Since it is an order of magnitude cheaper to capture the facsimile image, ADL recommends that a design study be initiated to develop software which recognises characters on documents stored as facsimile. If the study were successful, the software would be used at all ARTEMIS stores to create text from the facsimile data bases.

---

*See Glossary, under SBS

39

The cheapest way to load text into ARTEMIS stores would be to use the by-products of text preparation. Nearly all published material can be prepared on word or text processors (see Figure 3.4.A), and nearly all of these can store the printed characters on a machine-readable medium. The incremental cost is less than 1,000 ECUs per annum, much of which would be recovered in greater efficiency, per work station. Such a work station would have an annual throughput of about 1,000 pages if dedicated to a single typical journal and a capacity of 10,000 pages per annum if fully loaded. So a by-product 'tape' might cost as much as one ECU per page, which is not much more than copy typing, if installed merely to provide ARTEMIS input. However, a true by-product, from a system with the required hardware installed for other reasons, has a marginal cost of the order of 0.01 ECUs per page.

Host computer operators will have to develop procedures or standards for accepting texts on the wide range of common media, such as *diskettes, tape cartridges* and *'floppy disks'*, used in text and word processors. They should also be able to receive transmissions from communicating word processors.

ADL recommends the establishment of a joint information provider/ARTEMIS launch team working party to agree these standards and encourage the co-operation of manufacturers.

With microfilm archives, a major cost is checking that all pages have been microfilmed and that the standards of legibility have been maintained. This process requires a human inspector. In ARTEMIS, however, the vast majority of documents would be reproduced and sent to a reader soon after being stored, so prompt notification of sub-standard quality can be expected. Visual inspection can be confined to documents not requested within, say, three months, after which the source document may be difficult to retrieve for re-digitalising. Statistical quality control should be able to ensure economically that the reject rate is acceptably low.

FIGURE 3.4.A

TRADITIONAL AND AUTOMATED COMPOSITION PROCESSES

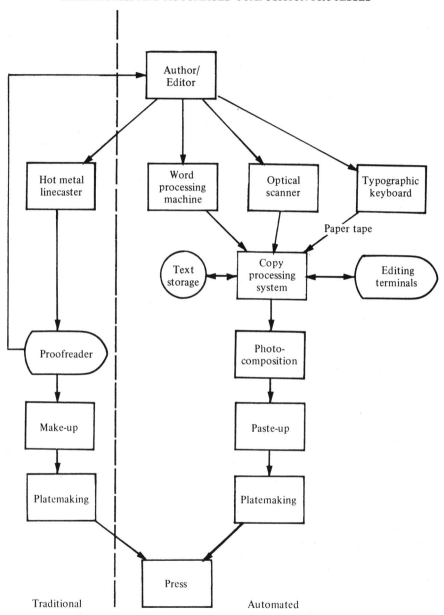

SOURCE: Arthur D. Little, Inc.

3.5 Summary of Costs of Document Capture and Storage

3.5.1 Document Capture

Figure 3.5.A shows the different routes by which documents reach the text and facsimile data bases. The tables below show the costs per page of stored document, with likely ranges, in hundredths of an ECU, for each process.

TELETEX
(Hundredths of an ECU)

Process	As by-product		By OCR	
	Min.	Max.	Min.	Max.
Transport to conversion centre	–		1	6
Preparation of bit stream	1	60	6	15
Transport to data base	1	6	1	6
Transmission to data base* (if necessary)	4	10	4	10
Edit, index, load	1	6	1	6
Storage cost	–	1	–	1

FACSIMILE
(Hundredths of an ECU)

Process	Min.	Max.
Transport to conversion centre	1	6
Reading by facsimile scanner	1	10
Transport to data base	1	6
Transmission to centre* (if necessary)	60	80
Edit, index, load	1	6
Storage cost	1	6

*Using Euronet at cheap rate, efficiently for small or large volumes

Not all steps in the complete process are required for every page, nor do the minima and maxima coincide. So the total cost per page has the following ranges:

				Min.	Max.
Total cost per page	– Teletex	–	By-product	10	70
		–	OCR	8	40
	– Facsimile			5	70

FIGURE 3.5.A

DOCUMENT CAPTURE AND STORAGE

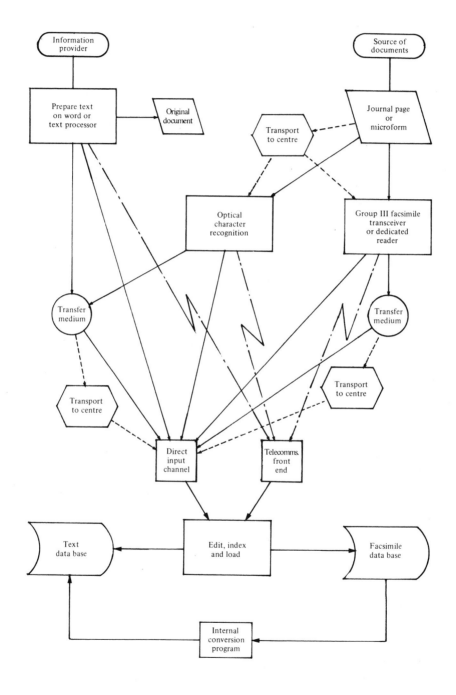

The process of editing, indexing and loading is difficult to cost because it will generally be one of many applications run in a host system. A hypothetical system dedicated to ARTEMIS might have a capital value for equipment and premises of one million ECUs and cost about 400,000 ECUs per annum to run. It would have a capacity to load, say, two million pages per annum and handle up to 10,000 requests, each for several pages, per night. (See Table 3.5.B.)

Here it is assumed that the data base hosts can achieve an edit, index and load cost of 0.01 - 0.10 ECUs per page.

The wide range between minimum and maximum costs makes the planner's task difficult. However, the variation reflects the real options that are open.

If all the processes take place at a large fulfilment centre, such as a national library, economies of scale can be achieved and physical movement and/or telecommunications avoided in the loading process. Dedicated, heavily used special purpose readers coupled to the computer can push the cost of OCR and facsimile down below 0.10 ECU per page.

An information provider who attaches his text processing data base directly to ARTEMIS can achieve a similar low cost.

In contrast, a host *(1)* receiving documents from a distant information provider by mail, over Euronet, or by facsimile on standard equipment which is little used, *(2)* maintaining appropriate software for a low volume activity and *(3)* using non-archival storage media, could incur much higher costs. These might be justified for data of special value, such as up-to-the-minute news.

For non-urgent documents, the following maxima apply (in ECUs per page):

Text as By-product	Text by OCR	Facsimile
0.70	0.30	0.30

3.5.2 Data Base to Data Base

One ARTEMIS data base can load itself from another, either by telecommunications or by a transfer medium like magnetic tape. This 'inter-library loan' or rather 'copying service', is economically justified if delivery to the end users involves a distance-dependent telecommunications charge, rather than a Euronet fixed rate, or if printing occurs at the site of the receiving store.

Major ARTEMIS data bases may be linked by leased telecommunications lines with low marginal costs and an average transmission charge per page of facsimile of less than 0.01 ECU. Such copies should cost about 0.03 ECU per page, well below the cost of digitalising the source document.

TABLE 3.5.B

HYPOTHETICAL LARGE DEDICATED ARTEMIS
FULFILMENT CENTRE AND STORE

	Teletex	**Facsimile**
Pages loaded, per annum	1,000,000	1,000,000
Data base, size in pages	10,000,000	10,000,000
Enquiry rate, pages per annum	5,000,000	5,000,000
Capital cost (ECU) of hardware, software and premises	1,000,000	
Annual costs (ECU):		
Amortisation of capital	200,000	
Maintenance (hardware, software)	50,000	
Operating staff	200,000	
Overheads	50,000	
Total	**500,000**	
Cost allocation (ECU)		
Loading cost	80,000	120,000
Fulfilment cost	120,000	180,000
Total cost	**200,000**	**300,000**
Cost per page fulfilled (ECU)	0.04	0.06

3.6   Document Receiving and Printing

ARTEMIS users can receive documents on a wide variety of terminals, which fall into two basic classes:

- Facsimile;
- Teletex

These terminals can be located: at the reader's desk; in a mailroom, printing office or copying facility in his own office building; at a commercial bureau; or at a fulfilment centre, such as a library. If the document is not produced at his desk, a messenger will have to transport it, resulting in delay and cost.

Large organisations will often accept streams of facsimile or teletex data over telecommunications lines directly into their computers, and store them on local memory for subsequent printing. Suitable computers vary from the largest machines to home computers with a serial communications interface and suitable modem.

Companies developing integrated electronic offices can connect their common data bases through their communications switches to Euronet and hence route the data stream to appropriate terminals.

Where large volumes of documents are involved, (even though many do not originate from ARTEMIS), the computers can print on peripheral devices based on traditional or new technologies:

- Impact:
  - Line printers;
  - Teleprinters;

- Thermal matrix;

- Ink jet;

- Laser;

- Intelligent copiers;

- Computer output microfilm.

Such equipment has high fixed and low variable costs per page and ranges in quality from just legible to original 'top copy' typing. Some non-impact devices (ink jet, laser, thermal matrix and intelligent copier) could be programmed to reproduce facsimile documents, although ADL is not aware of any currently being actively marketed. It is also possible to attach a facsimile receiver as a peripheral device to a computer. ADL recommends that the Commission invite proposals to develop the appropriate hardware and software.

Although more pages will be printed at big centres with expensive equipment, more users will have simple terminals for low volumes of facsimile or teletex.

The teletex terminals may be connected to the hosts (see Figure 3.6.A) via the public switched telephone network, a leased data line, a public switched data network or via Euronet, directly or through a suitable interface at the PTT node.

For connection over the data network, the forthcoming CCITT S Series recommendations for teletex apply. All such terminals will accept international alphabet number 5, and operate typically at 2,400 bits per second. Various other terminals can work through 'black boxes' which convert speeds and codes between standards.

Users receiving facsimile will have an increasing choice of machines conforming to CCITT Group 3 standards. New services from the PTTs and international carriers will promote the use of facsimile machines, so most users will not dedicate their equipment to ARTEMIS, but spread the cost of equipment over many documents.

Besides Group 3 machines, there are numerous slower Group 1 and Group 2 devices. Some ARTEMIS bureaux might offer speed and code translation from Group 3 to the slower machines. Such bureaux could be hosts, large fulfilment centres, commercial copying bureaux or in-house computer departments of user companies whose readers have slow fax receivers.

CCITT recommendation T.30 applies to facsimile transmission over the telephone network. CCITT is now studying Group 4 digital machines which will operate over public data networks. Recommendations will eventually follow and ARTEMIS would wish to adopt them promptly. Meanwhile, an interface between Group 3 machines and Euronet is required, either within the receiver, or at the PTT's Euronet node.

FIGURE 3.6.A **USER CONNECTIONS TO ARTEMIS HOSTS**

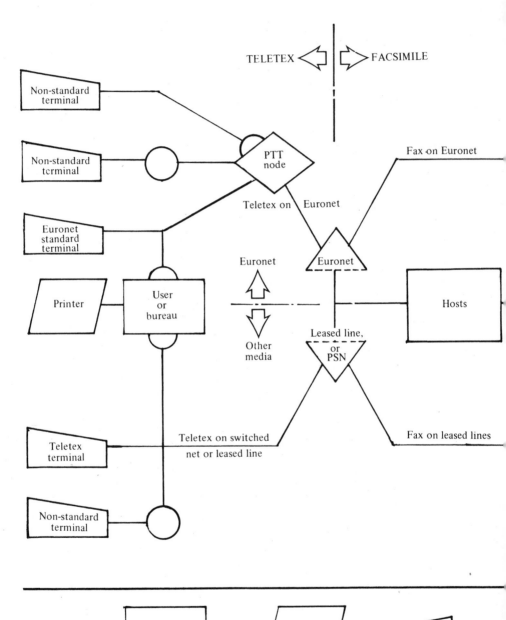

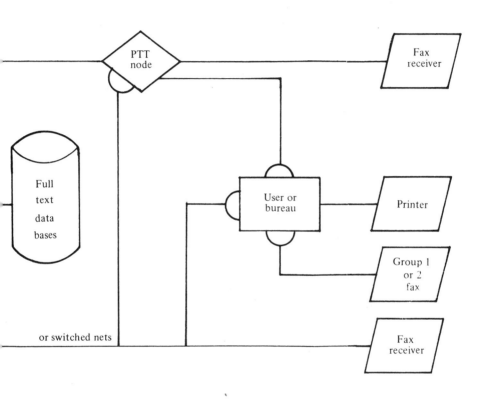

PTT node

Fax receiver

Full text data bases

User or bureau

Printer

Group 1 or 2 fax

or switched nets

Fax receiver

Speed and code convertor

Adaptor or interface

Data store

Node or switch on public network

3.7   Summary of Delivery and Printing Costs

The following figures assume that:

- A facsimile page contains 2.10^5 bits after data compression;

- A teletex page contains 2,000 characters which are transmitted in an eight-bit code, requiring 16,000 bits per page.

Transmission costs payable to the PTTs vary with the type of service used, and the choice of service will depend on volume, distance, and time of day. It will also depend on what other applications the user can run on the same communications links.

A large user relying on Euronet for 10,000 pages of facsimile per annum would pay about 0.60 ECUs per page. A small user, who uses Euronet for 1,000 pages of teletex per annum would pay about 0.10 ECUs for each. (See Table 3.1.A above.)

Big international private networks based on leased lines achieve costs of 0.02 ECUs to 0.15 ECUs for teletex pages and 0.20 to 2.0 ECUs for fax.

ADL studied the possibilites of satellite communication and concluded that costs an order of magnitude lower than those of leased lines were possible. However, PTT approval might not be forthcoming and the technology is not available and tested today. The PTTs might themselves incorporate satellite links and reduce their tariffs, particularly for international communication at night, within the next few years.

ADL recommended that the CEC approach the PTTs to consider an overnight file-to-file transfer tariff for Euronet which would allow fax pages to be sent for 0.20 ECUs and teletex pages for 0.05 ECU in small batches.

Having received the transmission, the user would require a terminal to print it. Small users will have capital costs of 2,000 to 10,000 ECUs for minimum capability equipment to receive teletex and facsimile respectively. These will need paper, supplies, operator attention and maintenance, following installation and connection.

A dedicated facsimile machine rented for 400 ECUs per month costs 15 ECUs per night and can receive 500 pages in a night shift at an average equipment cost of 0.03 ECUs cents per page. At 15 pages per night, or three per cent utilisation, the cost reaches 1.0 ECUs which may be unacceptably high. Paper and other costs add 0.03 to 0.06 ECUs per page.

A dedicated teleprinter at minimum cost, working at 1,200 bits per second, can accept 2,000 pages in an eight hour night shift at a capital cost of 2.00 ECUs per night, or 0.001 ECU per page. Paper costs are only a few cents (US), so even at a low utilisation of five per cent, the cost per page would be below 0.05 ECUs.

Taking equipment and transmission costs together for a large user, a minimum of 0.07 ECU for teletex and 0.30 ECUs for facsimile might be achieved, if a favourable tariff can be negotiated. (See Table 3.7.A.)

Many users will have less heavily utilised facilites and may pay up to 1.00 ECU for fax and 0.50 ECUs for teletex rather than use a bureau service and wait for delivery. Messenger services would charge several ECUs per order, and orders would generally contain few pages for users without the volume to justify their own equipment.

However, many users might have Euronet terminals (accepting only teletex*) for ordering, but have the facsimile documents transmitted to a nearby bureau or fulfilment centre for collection. Such centre would have high utilisation and low page costs of, say, 0.30 ECU and be able to charge twice as much.

For comparison, photocopies from DIALORDER (see Table 2.5.A above) cost from 0.30 ECUs per page by mail.

*Eventually, telex and teletex will interwork, allowing users to order by telex

TABLE 3.7.A

**TARGET DELIVERY AND PRINTING COSTS
FOR MATURE ARTEMIS SYSTEM**

(ECUs per page for small and large users)

	Teletex		Facsimile	
	Small	Large	Small	Large
PTT charges	0.10	0.05	0.50	0.20
User terminal	0.05	0.01	0.30	0.06
Supplies	0.01	0.01	0.05	0.04
Total	**0.16**	**0.07**	**0.85**	**0.30**

4. LEGAL, REGULATORY AND MANAGEMENT ISSUES

4.1 Telecommunications Regulations

The exclusive privilege and common carrier regulations of the European PTTs are now under review in the light of new technologies and services. There are pressures for harmonisation of regulations across Europe and for the lowering of both national and international tariffs.

ARTEMIS would not be significant to the PTTs for the revenue it will bring, but it might establish important precedents. Rather than negotiate a special status for ARTEMIS, which could delay the project, it would be better to build on Euronet and fit in with present practices.

The PTTs' active co-operation can be expected because ARTEMIS would:

- Occupy under-utilised facilities at night;
- Produce revenues of several million ECUs per annum to the PTT;
- Promote standards developed by CEPT and CCITT.

Accordingly, the CEC may be able to agree a low night-time file-to-file transfer tariff, or negotiate a bulk discount. Since communications costs are an important component of user charges for ARTEMIS, lower tariffs should encourage demand.

Analogies between ARTEMIS, the different national videotex systems (Prestel, Antiope and Bildschirmtext) and SWIFT should be drawn with caution. However, basing ARTEMIS on Euronet should create no difficulty with the definition of its service.

The PTTs can be expected to respond to a request for tenders for terminal equipment, such as facsimile receivers and teletex standard terminals. Their active participation in all parts of the pilot project should be invited, not just in the extension of the network.

ARTEMIS users would communicate with hosts over:

- Euronet;
- Public switched telephone network (PSTN);
- Public switched data network (PSDN);
- Leased data links.

Hosts will use the same services to exchange data with each other. All participants will need support from the PTTs, and the PTTs will want to encourage use not only of these services, but also of facilities such as multiplexers, switches, modems and speed and code conversion devices between one network and another. (An example is the connection of a start-stop terminal via the PSTN to a Euronet node.)

ARTEMIS management would want to work with the European Space Agency to demonstrate the feasibility of a full text retrieval service using OTS or ECS, once the pilot project has confirmed feasibility using a more conventional communications medium.

It is neither possible nor necessary at this time to predict the outcome of discussions with the PTTs about a hypothetical commercial service using one or more ground stations linked to ARTEMIS hosts, and a large number of small antennae on the users' premises to receive satellite transmissions. The PTTs may operate ground stations themselves, integrate satellite links into Euronet or add to their transmission capacity to remote areas in the future. But they will also be offering new fast circuit-switched data networks, and exploiting new switching and transmission technology during this decade. ARTEMIS users may benefit from an overall lowering of tariffs in line with the costs of new technology, rather than the cost of accumulated investment in today's network.

The success of ARTEMIS within Europe should lead to the export of the contents of its data bases and of appropriate terminals to other parts of the world. The PTTs would expect revenue from the international communications links as a result. Low tariffs in Europe will encourage rapid growth of ARTEMIS, attract export business more quickly and yield a return directly to the PTTs from foreign traffic. So ARTEMIS management will not be seeking a one-sided bargain from the PTTs.

4.2   Trans-border Data Flow and Data Protection

European countries are all working on, or have already enacted, data protection legislation. Such legislation generally has provisions for regulating the flow of information across national borders. The Council of Europe, the European Commission, the European Parliament and the Organisation for Economic Co-operation and Development are actively seeking harmonisation of data protection and trans-border data flow regulations to facilitate the free flow of information between nations whilst preserving individual rights.

Since ARTEMIS would provide a means of transferring information across borders, its operations will be subject to such regulations as have or may be instituted. Where a data protection authority licences the operation of systems, it can be presumed that ARTEMIS would be permitted to operate without significant restraints. In different countries within Europe, the registered responsible party may be the information provider, the operator of the host computer, or users, individually or as a consortium.

Conditions of the licence might require that name-linked data which are not derived directly from printed publications, should not be transmitted. Such rules might apply to judicial persons as well as identifiable individuals. So the distribution across borders of dossiers about legal and physical persons, or even building of data bases of published material about them, may be subject to some restriction.

There may also be requirements to ensure the secrecy of files identifying the materials sought by individuals or organisations. It may well be possible to deduce from the requests fulfilled by an ARTEMIS centre precisely which topics interest a particular organisation.

ARTEMIS would contribute to the development of a free trade area for information products and is therefore congruent with the overall objectives of the European community. Information will, however, be traded outside the Community, both with other OECD countries, and with the developing world and Communist countries. Some of the information will have a strategic value and maybe subject to COCOM, the International Co-ordinating Committee of NATO and some other nations, which tries to prevent the transfer of technology useful to the development of armaments to potential enemies. There may therefore be restrictions on what may be stored in the ARTEMIS data bases and on who may have access to them.

Other restrictions may apply to pornographic material, descriptions of technology of value to terrorists (such as bomb making, and biological or chemical weapons) and even the advertising of products (such as pharmaceuticals or narcotics) which are banned.

The less developed countries have called for a New International Information Order comparable with the New International Economic Order that they seek. They want a free and balanced flow of information between nations and wish to reduce their dependence on foreign sources of information and information technology. Europeans, too, have recognised that it is possible to be too dependent on foreign sources of vital information, not least in the fields of science and technology. Individual countries within Europe may not wish to have data vital to their economies, judicial processes or defence, located outside their own jurisdiction, with the attendant risk that they might be cut off from them.

At the same time, the owners of the intellectual property associated with the information resource, which is being traded like any other commodity, will wish to ensure that their interests are protected, not only in their own countries, but wherever their property is stored.

ARTEMIS will bring many of these issues to a head and may therefore provide a valuable catalyst to speed up the work on the development of the relevant international agreements, in which European institutions are taking a leading role.

4.3 Intellectual Property

ADL was specifically instructed not to consider the important issues of copyright, since these are the subject of on-going work elsewhere. However, we did undertake to identify any new issues raised by our proposals for those involved in the study of intellectual property.

We would therefore draw their attention to the following points:

• There may be many versions of the same text, such as a black and white facsimile, colour facsimile, a low resolution version, a *formatted* and *unformatted* character string version, stored in many different places within the ARTEMIS system;

• A full text data base can in principle be searched and material of intellectual value can be extracted without printing the whole of it;

• Excerpts, abstracts, translations and other spin-offs can be prepared by computer, or by a human editor with computer assistance;

• New compendia can be created, containing complete texts or excerpts;

• Text can be read without printing, by using VDUs or videotex equipment;

• The end user or his information intermediary (such as in-house librarian) can receive a single transmission from ARTEMIS, but make many prints of it.

We have recommended that the pilot project for ARTEMIS should be developed around a data base of material that does not raise copyright and related issues. However, these issues must be resolved before the full potential of ARTEMIS can be realised.

4.4   Impact on Stakeholder Interests

ARTEMIS improves the information market place and promotes the supply of computer-backed information systems and data. It therefore affects all the partners in the information industry. (See Table 4.4.A.)

The users will have access to information more quickly and more easily, and sometimes more cheaply. The CEC, as sponsors of ARTEMIS, can expect the users to support the initiative, but must recognise a problem already identified by Viewdata's promoters: users will not invest in high cost capital equipment unless the range and quality of information is sufficient to create an adequate volume of traffic to spread the cost of equipment.

The suppliers of services (hosts and PTTs) and products (such as terminals), have much to gain from larger markets and increased equipment utilisation. So active support can be expected on such matters as:

●   Night tariffs for file-to-file transfers;
●   Standard terminals at reasonable cost;
●   Software and interface development;
●   Response to request for tenders for special equipment, such as digitalisers;
●   Participation in standards working parties.

Authors and publishers will benefit from new distribution channels, provided that their intellectual property is protected appropriately. However, there may be some loss of formality in scholarly publishing.

Printers and booksellers, who today deal with information on paper, may find a wider market and may well diversify to become public fulfilment centres, like high street copying bureaux, linked to ARTEMIS and supporting a mass of small users who cannot afford their own equipment.

ADL urges the CEC to encourage the representatives of all the interest groups to attack the new market created by ARTEMIS, not to defend their traditional corners.

Librarians in particular, as custodians of valuable archives today and as providers of information services to a growing community, should play a leading role in promoting ARTEMIS as a key component of the infrastructure of tomorrow's information economy.

The CEC itself will want to help stakeholders adjust to the changes so that the benefits for the majority are not achieved at crippling expense to a few. So the ARTEMIS pilot project must be accompanied by consultation with and support for those whose prosperity depends on today's technology.

TABLE 4.4.A

STAKEHOLDERS IMPACTED BY ARTEMIS

AUTHORS

Literary agents
Editors
Referees
Indexes
Photographers and artists

PRINTERS

Compositors
Platemakers
Binders

PUBLISHERS

Technical and learned societies
Information brokers
Data base owners
Spinners
Distributors — mail and transport

BOOKSELLERS

Wholesalers
Tearsheets
Secondhand

LIBRARIES

Information intermediaries

USERS

Consultants

SERVICES AND PRODUCTS

PTTs
Computer hosts
Value added network operators
Equipment manufacturers

4.5 Standards

Ultimately, all that would remain of ARTEMIS would be a set of agreed standards for the interchange of information between providers and users. Through the proper definition of these standards, a *conduit* will be created through which the full *content* can pass.

There would be no purely ARTEMIS standards, but ARTEMIS may be a catalyst for the more rapid development of other standards. All the necessary standards either exist today or have been proposed. It is probable that additional standards, beyond those necessary for a pilot project, would be developed, particularly for the control of high quality printing and colour reproduction.

Within DG III (Internal Market and Industrial Affairs) of the CEC, there is a working group on standardisation − harmonisation in informatics (WGS-HI). It is Community policy to encourage the development of suitable standards both within ISO and the European standardisation bodies, and then to require suppliers of goods and services to conform to any such standards recommended by the community. WGS-HI encourages the production of standards, organises support for them, and makes them easier to use. It is recommended that DG XIII and DG III jointly establish a working party to define standards for ARTEMIS.

These standards should recognise that ARTEMIS is an *open system*, in which any user of the system has the ability to communicate with any other user of the system, regardless of who owns or supplies the equipment involved. ISO/TC97/SC16 is developing standards for the interconnection of open systems. They are elaborating an architectural model which defines the areas in which standards are needed. This model defines seven levels (see Figure 4.5.A) of which the lowest four constitute a *transport service*. Wherever applicable, the CCITT standards should be used within ARTEMIS. ARTEMIS stores will always use such transport services to deliver documents.

The computers of the ARTEMIS network and the terminals at the printing centre have to process the data as well as transmit them to each other. The upper three layers, application, presentation and session, have still to be defined, but work is well advanced in ISO on file-to-file transfer protocols of the type required by ARTEMIS. The computer application of finding a full text, preparing it in suitable format for delivery to the distant terminal, and ensuring that it is printed out correctly involves *opening* and *closing sessions* between the central system and the user, and manipulating the data appropriately for presentation. ARTEMIS may well pioneer the development of the appropriate high level protocols.

The standards are defined, not in terms of what the components of the system do, but of the information that they interchange. Figure 4.5.B shows the interfaces across which the information being exchanged within ARTEMIS must move. The standards that are needed include those listed in Table 4.5.C.

FIGURE 4.5.A

ISO PROVISIONAL ARCHITECTURAL MODEL

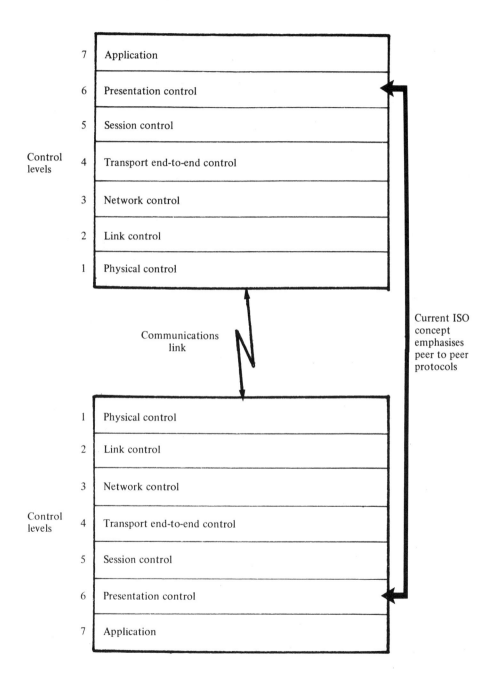

FIGURE 4.5.B

INTERFACES REQUIRING STANDARDS

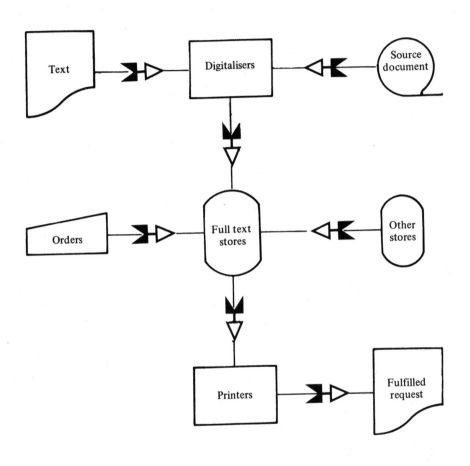

62

TABLE 4.5.C

PARTIAL LIST OF STANDARDS APPLICABLE TO ARTEMIS

ISO	2382	Data processing vocabulary
	2375	Escape sequence registration
CCITT	V4	7-bit character representation for data transmission
	V3	International alphabet number 5
ISO	2022	Code extension techniques
	/DP 4873	8-bit coded character set
ECMA	5,12,36	Data interchange on magnetic tape
ISO	3275	Data interchange on magnetic cassette
ECMA	13,41	Tape labels and file structures
ISO	/DP 5654	Data interchange on flexible disk
CCITT	V24, X24	DTE/DCE interface definitions
	X20, X21, X25	DTE/DCE interface characteristics
	V24	Code independent data transfer
ANS	Z39.2	Bibliographic information interchange on magnetic tape
	Z39.5	Abbreviation of titles of periodicals
	Z39.21	Book numbering
	Z39.29	Bibliographic references
ISO	2784	Computer stationery sizes and formats
	2530	Keyboard layouts
	1004	Character recognition codes
ECMA	42	Character set for matrix printers
CCITT	T Series	Apparatus and transmission for facsimile telegraphy

The host computers supporting the ARTEMIS data bases may be used for many other different applications as well. ARTEMIS would place no requirements on the host to provide any particular form of hardware or software. However, it may be useful to develop a standard format for the information stored *within* the system, in order to avoid unnecessary conversion from one format to another when exchanging data *between* hosts. The files of information being transferred into, and being transferred out of, an ARTEMIS store must be self-defining, so that they distinguish themselves from other files of information being handled by the same host computer. Within the host however, it is the operator's responsibility to store and retrieve the data, using whatever storage medium he prefers. The operator can in principle choose any compaction scheme and encryption method he likes, but at the cost of having to decode and expand the bit streams before transmitting them to other stores. It is recommended therefore that ARTEMIS adopt a standard compaction algorithm for transmission, and does not use encryption for most transmitted data since they are in any case available in printed form. It seems appropriate to use the CCITT Group 3 facsimile compaction algorithm as a standard. This avoids speed and code conversion on input and output, and thus reduces the processing load, but still permits additional compaction and expansion, if the operator wishes, between the main memory and the archives themselves. (See Table 3.3.A above.)

Speed and code conversion, however, are both possible and necessary, in particular for communicating with cheaper terminals. ARTEMIS hosts will offer a range of interfaces to user terminals, including Group 3 facsimile and teletex. They may also offer videotex, telex, and proprietory standards such as IBM's EBCDIC and SDLC. (Proprietory standards would not be part of the open ARTEMIS system, but host computers may be members of other systems, such as DIANE, as well as members of ARTEMIS. Users will connect with hosts through ports which support the speeds and codes appropriate to their terminals. By definition, every ARTEMIS host would have to have at least one port which operates according to ARTEMIS standards.)

For facsimile, the CCITT recommendation TO (1976) will apply. This defines Group 3 apparatus which uses digital techniques and incorporates means for reducing redundant information in the document signal prior to the modulation process. The details are specified in recommendation T4 which is currently in draft form but which should be ratified at the CCITT Plenary assembly this year. This standard applies only to black and white facsimile. A full A4 document takes less than a minute to be transmitted. A fourth group of equipment for use on public switched data networks, which incorporates appropriate error control techniques, has also been defined.

CCITT is studying an improved telex service, called teletex. This uses a more extensive character set than telex (which is limited to upper case) and is intended to meet the PTT's requirements for electronic mail. It should be capable of interworking with the telex service, which implies that ARTEMIS too could receive orders and deliver by telex, if the limited character set were acceptable. Again, the 1980 Plenary assembly of CCITT should lead to the appropriate agreements, in time for ARTEMIS to adopt the standards. The teletex terminal will comprise a keyboard, printer, storage facilities and communications interface.

Videotex will be outside ARTEMIS, but there is no reason why the two networks should not interwork. In principle, both are open systems and can have an interface at which speed and code conversion takes place. Videotex uses a modified television set and a keyboard to provide interactive data transmission across the public switched telephone network. CCITT and CEPT are looking at the possibilities of standardisation and interworking between different national systems.

The alphabet or code used by ARTEMIS for the exchange of character data should be based on ISO 646:1973, seven-bit coded character set for information processing interchange, and its close relative ISO 4783:1979 eight-bit coded character sets for information interchange.

ARTEMIS will have to develop a numbering plan analogous to telephone numbers, since the open system permits any user to approach any host. CCITT has made provisional recommendation X 121 (1978) for an international numbering plan for public data networks. This should form the basis of the ARTEMIS numbering plans.

The rules for encryption and error protection should be determined by the transport service, not by the ARTEMIS applications which use it. However, there may be non-ARTEMIS full text delivery services supporting closed user groups which operate mutually agreed encryption or error protection standards.

It will be necessary to use a standard bibliographic reference by means of which a user can identify uniquely the document he wishes the fulfilment centre to deliver. It is the responsibility of an ARTEMIS host to convert from the standard bibliographic reference to the internal key required to locate the document within his files. Appropriate standards already exist, but ADL recommend that a working party be established to define the ARTEMIS standard unambiguously and quickly.

The quality of the document ultimately provided to the reader depends on the quality of the original document stored at the host computer, the fidelity with which the host transmits to the user, the communications line and the receiving terminals. The information providers, who may be publishers, have an interest in maintaining quality along every link of the chain to the ultimate user and may feel that 'type-approval' for receiving terminals will be good for their image in the marketplace. However, we do not believe that ARTEMIS should take on a role comparable with that of the PTTs in defining standards for, and approving types of, terminals.

4.6   Pricing Policy

ARTEMIS is a marketplace, not a regulated utility, so it should not publish a tariff to which all hosts and information providers should conform. Nevertheless, the CEC will wish to ensure that users get quick and economical access to information on a non-discriminatory basis, an objective they sought with Euronet/DIANE also.

The ARTEMIS pilot project would establish the pricing policy, so ADL recommends that a working party should start promptly to determine it. Its suggestions include:

- A charge to the user for communications costs from the fulfilment centre to his terminal;

- A fixed fee per order, given that a correct citation is provided in an on-line order;

- A variable charge for the information provider's intellectual property;

- A fixed charge per page for the host's costs of digitalising and storage;

- No charge to the first user for digitalisation, (to encourage the growth of the data base);

- A search fee for non-digitalised material, by negotiation with the user;

- A citation correction service fee, for sorting out obscure, incomplete or confused references.

The components of this schedule for the pilot project should be based on the long range marginal costs of a successful service. It follows that start-up costs should be met by the CEC as promoters of the service.

The target price for the user for material not involving a copyright fee should be, in ECUs:

Cost Component		Teletex	Facsimile
Per order		0.70	0.70
Per page	— communications	0.10	0.50
	— host charges	0.05	0.07

In addition, the user would have to pay for his terminal and any transport of paper from terminal to reader.

When there are many hosts and data bases, fulfilment centres will have to agree a fee for copying from one data base to another.

The revenue to ARTEMIS hosts from fulfilling in a year:

- One million orders;
- Ten million pages;

would be 1.3 million ECU. This must pay for:

- Digitalising one million pages;
- Storing 2.10^{11} bits, with duplicates in several hosts;
- Retrieving one million orders.

The revenue to the PTTs will be about three million ECUs.

The users will pay about four million ECUs for one million orders averaging ten pages each, plus the cost of terminals and fees for copyright to the information providers.

4.7   Accounting

The accounting system must reflect the pricing policy, but is operated entirely by the hosts. The pilot project host must develop software and procedures which record:

- User identity and account number;
- Delivery address (i.e. receiving terminal);
- Service charges for incomplete orders or searches;
- Correct citation;
- Copyright fee for this citation;
- Format of delivery (facsimile or teletex);
- Host providing digitalised text;
- Copying charge from host to fulfilment centre;
- Referral fee from fulfilment centre to host;
- Communications medium used;
- PTT charges or private line charge;
- Number of pages ordered/delivered;
- Time and date of receipt of orders;
- Time and date of despatch;
- User balance with fulfilment centre.

Users may maintain accounts with several fulfilment centres, or choose to work always through a single centre. In either case, the fulfilment centre accepting the order would be responsible for:

- Billing the user and getting paid;
- Payments to hosts;
- Payments to PTTs;
- Fees for copyright to information providers.

(Note that ADL was not asked to consider either the principles or mechanics of copyright payments; both must be resolved before ARTEMIS can be developed beyond a pilot project.)

4.8   Locating Documents

The document location index to the total ARTEMIS collection would ultimately contain tens of millions of entries with pointers to hundreds of millions of items, since there will be duplicates and versions of documents in different data bases.

For the pilot project, there would be only one such index* located at the single host. Before the pilot project expands to more hosts and data bases, something like an "ARTEMIS location index working party" must decide how to index the whole collection.

There are two possible approaches, with variants within them:

● Central;
● Distributed.

With a central location index in a host computer linked to Euronet, each addition to the data base at any host would generate an update to the index. The hosts would create the citations and send them directly to the index system operator over Euronet or by leased telecommunications links.

Each fulfilment centre, on receiving an order, would check its own index. On failing to find the document in its own collection, it would forward the order to the central index which would acknowledge it and route it to a host with a data base containing the document, according to an established priority list. It would also indicate whether the original fulfilment centre wants to buy a copy to add to its own data base, or requires the request to be fulfilled by direct delivery to the user.

A distributed location index can be in two forms:

● Completely distributed to hosts;
● Partially distributed with union indexes for groups of hosts.

The operation of a distributed index system begins with the fulfilment centre, which takes the order, checking its own collection. Failing to find the item it can either:

● Broadcast to all other centres;

● Attach to the order an address list of hosts to be tried in sequence and send it the first one on the list;

● Pass the order to a 'specialist host' which will 'ring up' hosts to try to find the item.

---

*The location index referred to here should not be confused with a subject index. (See Glossary.)

Broadcasting is expensive, but may be an appropriate last resort. The specialist host may be expert in only one area, and be kept informed (i.e. hold a partial central index) by other hosts of the collections in his area of interest. Some countries might establish such an index for their national collections.

With the address list approach, the request goes to each addressee in turn. Each addressee checks his own index, and passes the request on, deleting his own address (and adding others to the end of the list if the first centre is willing to pay for such help) if he cannot fulfill it.

The operators of bibliographic data bases will need access to these location indices, whether centralised or distributed, to check their own bibliographic references and to advise their own customers about the availability of documents.

5.   THE LIKELY DEVELOPMENT OF ARTEMIS

5.1   Services to be Provided

From the beginning, ARTEMIS should have the same geographical extent as DIANE, since both use Euronet. A user will send a standard bibliographic reference to a host computer on which is loaded an ARTEMIS full text data base. He will identify his own terminal and receive overnight either a teletex version or a facsimile version of the text on terminals which conform to the appropriate standard.

The initial data base will be limited, almost certainly to one subject area and to less than 100,000 items, and the user community will also be limited initially.

As more and more data bases are added, additional hosts participate, more users join in, then new services, such as colour facsimile, Group 1 and 2 facsimile, rush delivery, on-line searching and browsing, will be developed.

5.2   The Full Text Stores

Documents within ARTEMIS are in the form of strings of bits, organised in a standard format, either facsimile or teletex. In the former case, each page of information requires about 200,000 bits; in the latter, 16,000 would suffice.

Once information has been converted into a bit-string it can be stored on conventional data processing media, such as magnetic disks and tapes, or on the new and less familiar optical storage media. Optical disks and tapes are well suited to archival storage of material that will not change, since the data are stored indelibly. This contrasts with magnetic media, which can be erased and re-written any number of times; magnetic as well as optical media have the ability to be read any number of times.

Any computer centre with an interface to Euronet has the capability to become an ARTEMIS archival store. As with DIANE the host and the data base are logically independent. The information provider makes use of the host computer and the network to provide a conduit by means of which he delivers the content of the data base to the user. The providers of content and conduit can be quite independent.

ARTEMIS would eventually comprise a large number of archival stores, each containing a data base and a computer system which can find the information and prepare it for transmission and/or printing. Although the format of the data would conform to an ARTEMIS standard, at least on entering and leaving the host computer, different operators will choose different media on which to store the data bases. Very large data bases may have dedicated computer systems, or be attached to computers only at night when no other applications are running. Small data bases will share a host and some of them may be on-line during the day. Information providers and hosts would operate in a marketplace just like the owners of and hosts for bibliographic data bases. By conforming to the ARTEMIS standards, both of them could reach a wide user market.

Information could be sent from one store to another and each store would have to determine, possibly by reference to common ARTEMIS conventions or to bilateral agreements, whether it will keep a copy of information it has received from another store, or merely retain the inform-ation for long enough to fulfill a request. Some publishers may maintain archives of their own material, either on their own machines or on a host's, and would fulfill requests by sending the data to users directly. It is also likely that some libraries would establish full text stores based on their own collections, and have an inter-library updating service, whereby each library would send to its fellows any newly digitalised documents which fit in with their interest profiles. ARTEMIS should encourage both kinds of developments.

Each host would have to maintain an index to the data base it holds and be capable of converting a standard bibliographic reference into a key by means of which it could find the text to fulfill the request. The necessary software for this application is readily available and presents no particular problems.

Each store would keep the data at the highest resolution necessary to fulfill requests. For teletex information, an eight-bit code would be used to permit the handling of all standard characters in each of the European languages. For facsimile, a resolution of eight lines per millimetre would be stored. For facsimile data, compression is normal and the CCITT standard defines the appropriate algorithm. The host system operator would be free to choose a different algorithm, or to encypher his data, but there seems to be no reason why he should.

With the teletex data also, compression would be possible but there is no standard algorithm. Furthermore, the volumes would be much less than for facsimile and the standard form of transmission would not involve *companding*. Some hosts may decide to save space, others may decide not to use processing power to compress and expand during storage and retrieval.

As the system approaches maturity, ARTEMIS would involve a large number of hosts of various sizes and a wide variety of data bases. The same text may appear in many different data bases if the information provider agrees. (The index to a public data base must be public, so information providers can always determine who is offering their data.) The data bases will vary in size from a few hundred documents to many million. Hosts would be able to use a variety of technologies, including some as yet untried, to provide the physical storage. Cost of storage is going down rapidly as shown in Figure 3.2.B (above). It will always be cheaper to store a document in digital form once it has been digitalised, than to repeat the digitalisation process. Furthermore, it is cheaper to get a digitalised version from another store and add it to one's own, provided the information provider agrees, than to undertake the manual process of digitalisation. Finally, adding to store is cheaper than delivering to the user, so the user is mainly concerned with delivery cost. However, storage may cost the host more than locating the document and processing it ready for transmission. So the host would have an incentive to run his store efficiently.

5.3   Adding Documents to Stores

ARTEMIS would contain two distinct classes of documents, those for delivery by teletex and those for delivery by facsimile. Secondly, there would be two distinct sources of documents: an already printed page (or microform), and a by-product tape from a text processing operation. Information from the by-product tape would be stored in teletex format. The other input medium can be converted by optical character recognition into teletex format or by facsimile scanning into a standard Group 3 digital bit-stream. The document delivered to the user by facimile would be very nearly identical to the original and would have exactly the same layout. However, the text delivered by teletex may have different line lengths, character sets, page make-up and so on.

In principle, it would be possible to establish standards that would enable a text stored for teletex delivery to contain formatting instructions, type font selection characters and various other characters which would make it possible for the provider of a document for delivery by teletex to determine the format in which it will ultimately be printed. ARTEMIS may indeed facilitate the development of the appropriate standards, but it is not possible that they could be ready in time for the start-up of the service.

Providers of information for the teletex service would deliver data in the appropriate format and on a suitable medium to the host for loading to the data base. It would be up to the information provider and the host to agree on acceptable media, such as cassettes, diskettes, magnetic card, paper tape or telecommunications link, and who will convert the by-product of text editing into standard form by removing control characters and so on. The text to be stored must conform to the teletex standard currently being determined by ISO and CCITT. The relationship between information provider and host will determine whether the information provider is buying a service from the host, or the host is buying data for his data base from the information provider. One host may have many providers and one provider may use many hosts. (These are the circumstances under which de facto standards generally arise, and the EEC would wish to encourage this.)

Using by-product tapes from text processing works satisfactorily for text and for a limited range of alphabets, including, for example, mathematical symbols, but it cannot handle diagrams and photographs. For non-text information and for much existing material, facsimile scanning is the preferred technique. The source document, which might be a book, pages from a journal or a microform, will be scanned to convert the image on paper to a digital bit-stream from which the image can be recreated subsequently elsewhere. This technique preserves the format of the original, copes with pictures and requires much less development of standards since the CCITT has already proposed the appropriate formats for digital facsimile. The string of data bits can be compressed without losing information. This helps to keep the cost of storage and transmission down, but a page of information captured by facsimile methods will still require 10 to 100 times more bits of data than the equivalent information captured from the keyboard. (Essentially, the facsimile process has to have enough information to record the shape of a letter, whereas the capture of keystrokes merely has to identify the letter to be printed, not its shape.)

There are no standards yet for colour facsimile, although the technology exists, and the Group 3 standard does not provide for half-tones. Groups of information providers and users would be able to establish mutually acceptable standards for colour transmission, converting ARTEMIS into a distributed store-and-forward colour facsimile system. Such developments would be outside the basic service, but worthy of encouragement.

Existing material which contains only text can be read by OCR techniques. The individual letters are recognised by the computer controlled reading system and a short digital code is stored for each letter. In effect, this recaptures the keystrokes and can produce a digital bit-string which is logically equivalent to the keystrokes captured from new text. OCR devices can now handle a wide variety of type fonts and can work from paper or microform. However, multifont readers are either extremely expensive or very slow, and the technique is unlikely to find favour, except perhaps, for typewritten material, such as theses or reports.

Although no equipment is currently offered, the technology is now available to recognise characters in a digital facsimile. A computer could produce a string of teletex from the facsimile data base, therefore.

Ultimately, ARTEMIS would provide two distinct services: teletex and facsimile. The former will accept information prepared deliberately in text format, which was never intended for printing except at ARTEMIS terminals. The latter will deal with everything else, either because it started as a paper document, or because it contains non-text information. A hybrid system will grow, providing pairs of documents, one containing text and the other containing all the images associated with it. However, necessary standards could not be developed in the short term.

5.4   Printing Centres

In the ARTEMIS pilot project, a few organisations with Euronet terminals would add facsimile machines, and vice versa, so they can order and receive documents in either format. Most of these machines would be located in mail, telex or copier rooms not far from users' offices.

Experiments with the coupling of computers to Euronet to receive documents in digital form can begin immediately. Thus some organisations would be able to establish their computers as ARTEMIS output devices and would distribute facsimiles and teletex documents as they now distribute computer printout.

Among these computer-based printing centres may be some computer service bureaux, and even small copy bureaux with mini-computers dedicated to ARTEMIS. They will serve a clientele by messenger or across the counter. Big fulfilment centres, possibly based on major libraries, as well as ARTEMIS hosts, would also be printing centres.

The biggest centres will operate high capital cost, high quality equipment at low cost per page. Page printers with suitable software are very appropriate, but teletex will often be produced on conventional line printers. As ARTEMIS grows, manufacturers, large users and bureaux would develop the necessary minor modifications to conventional hardware and software. At the same time, facsimile machine manufacturers would develop interfaces to computers so that a receiver can work as a computer peripheral.

The majority of users would continue to use standard facsimile receivers which can operate unattended overnight, attached either to the telephone network, to Euronet, or later, to a public switched data network. These machines would be used for non-ARTEMIS traffic as well.

As teletex terminals become available, and as suppliers offer more virtual terminals for Euronet, these would be applied to ARTEMIS occasionally, or perhaps dedicated full time or overnight to receiving text. Domestic computers, word processors, and eventually, the data switches of integrated electronic offices would also be attached to the networks, sometimes by 'black boxes' to convert codes and speeds.

ARTEMIS would place only minimal restrictions on users' equipment. To 'sign on', the user would have to enter an agreement with at least one fulfilment centre to pay for the service, and undertake to respect the copyright of documents he receives. He will need to identify the protocols observed by his terminal and the network to which he is attached.

Users who are both big printing centres and hosts may want to keep copies of documents sent via them to fulfill clients' requests. Their agreements must be with other hosts, who in turn will have agreements with information providers about allowing copies to he held by more than one host. (Material that requires updating, like product lists, may have to be kept on a single host.)

5.5   Communications

Table 5.5.A shows all the transmission processes in ARTEMIS. The first movement of data is from the digitaliser to the host computer for loading into its data base. Much of this would be done in anticipation of user requests, so machine-readable media acceptable to the host will be created by the information provider. Some information will be created at the host on his computer; other documents will be digitalised by the information provider, or by a service bureau on his behalf, and sent by data link (Euronet, a leased line or a switched public network) to the host. The choice of method is entirely a matter between host and information provider.

Store-to-store transmission would be regulated by ARTEMIS hosts' agreements to respect copyright, update indexes and pay for copies of documents in each others' data bases. Stores which exchange large volumes of data may lease lines between them, while less regular correspondents would use Euronet or a public switched network. Some information providers may routinely send new documents to many stores, rather as newspapers are sent to news-stands, using one host to broadcast to the others.

The stores would have ports to Euronet, leased lines, the public switched data and telephone networks, and ultimately, perhaps, to a satellite ground station. User terminals will be attached to one or more of these transmission media to receive teletex or facsimile digital data streams, and will operate unattended, answering calls automatically. The user will choose the network, since he pays the charges, according to the volume of traffic he expects and the number and distance of the fulfilment centres he expects to use regularly. For the pilot project, Euronet would be used for all teletex delivery and for order entry. Facsimile delivery will be possible over any network available to the user, provided his receiver has a suitable interface.

As ARTEMIS develops, numerous speed and code conversion services and devices would be offered to users with non-standard equipment. Some will be 'black boxes' placed between the terminal and the network; others will be located at network nodes, switches or concentrators, or at hosts so the user can connect to them and receive a stream of data appropriate to his terminal.

The last stage of the document's journey to the reader would be generally by messenger or mail, either internal or external. However, some documents may be printed out at a big centre and transmitted by slow but cheap facsimile to the user.

TABLE 5.5.A

TRANSMISSION METHODS FOR ARTEMIS

	Digitaliser to store	Store to store	Store to terminal	Terminal to user
Physical transport of paper				*
Physical transport of machine readable media	*	x	x	
Teletransmission on leased lines or in bulk	x	*	x	
Teletransmission over switched network	x	x	*	
Teletransmission by broadcasting (one to many)	x	x	x	
Non-standard media (videotex, Group 1 Fax etc.)			x	x

Key:
* preferred method
x possible method

5.6   System Performance

The user's measures of system performance will be document quality, speed of delivery and ease of use.

Document quality is determined by the user's own terminal equipment and the digitalisation process. For facsimile, the standards are set by CCITT Group 3, and should be met easily by the equipment used for digitalising. For teletex, correct transmission of the character stream from store to terminal can be guaranteed, but there may be errors in the entered data, depending on the source: OCR may be unreliable with some type fonts; by-product tapes may not discriminate, for example, between subscripts and superscripts.

Correct orders reaching the fulfilment centre from the user by 18.00 hours on one day should be fulfilled by the following morning at 07.00 if the document exists in digitalised form anywhere in ARTEMIS. Documents not yet digitalised must be found and digitalised, which will normally require at least one more working day even when the user or fulfilment centre knows where the document can be found.

Users will require training to use ARTEMIS, although those who know DIANE need little more than a handbook. Reliable terminals which operate unattended are essential, and available from suppliers now. Search and citation correction services will be important adjuncts, and clear, unambigious standards must be developed.

APPENDICES

November, 1979

81

TABLE OF CONTENTS

1. CAPTURE TECHNIQUES FOR NEW MATERIAL

New material for publication is today usually captured in magnetic form utilising state-of-the-art micro, mini and large mainframe computers. Depending upon the system, the magnetic media used include: magnetic tape, disks, diskettes, cassettes and magnetic cards. At present, the only form of storage that regularly conforms to a standard is the magnetic tape.

Disks, diskettes, cassettes and magnetic cards have formats that vary from one vendor to another. The actual text data utilise either EBCDIC or ASCII character codes, but positional commands and text formatting and highlighting codes vary tremendously. Although it is feasible to capture most of the data on magnetic tape, the actual format codes have to accord with a standard defined by the vendor of the composing system. Only recently have these vendors offered the capability to interface to the various word processing equipments.

This section will present an overview of the three most appropriate types of systems: word processing, text processing and photocomposition.

1.1 Word Processing

The recent technological advances in miniaturisation of computers (micro-processors) and associated peripheral logic have made the concept of automatic text processing an attractive and economical means of producing various office documents locally. Although small and quite inexpensive relative to data processing systems, this equipment contains sophisticated micro- and mini-computer hardware augmented with software, in which many man-years of work have been invested. This software performs a variety of text creation and editing functions interactively.

There are at least 150 word processing systems offered by more than 50 vendors in the United States and nearly as many in Europe. Because of the multi-billion dollar potential market, large firms such as IBM, Exxon, AM International, DEC and Burroughs, have invested substantial development effort in these products and have created a highly competitive atmosphere.

1.1.1 Purpose of Word Processing System

Word processing equipment is designed to increase the efficiency or productivity of the office function — i.e. the production of various documents, document accessing via computer indexing and inter-/intra-department communications. The main purpose of this equipment is:

- To capture original keystrokes of rough draft text on storage devices;
- To provide text editing/modifications;
- To perform operations to increase efficiency;
- To produce typewriter-like quality automatically.

Depending upon the particular product and for an appropriate price, word processors can provide such features as hyphenation, justification, automatic search and replace, text merging, stored formats, document indexing, pagination, block move, delete and insert, and automatic word wrapping.

The general trend in word processors is to offer more capabilities — i.e. easier editing, output to camera-ready material for printing, more storage, faster response times.

1.1.2   Current Industry Applications

Word processors are primarily applied in paper-intensive industries where correspondence and documentation is required to support each transaction. Typical applications are found in insurance, hospitals, law firms and banking, as well as publishing.

While the initial impetus for the introduction of word processing has been to eliminate redundant keyboarding by secretaries, the major incentive will be, in our judgement, the opportunity for secretaries, copy editors and even authors to participate in a communications network which provides them access to a manuscript or data base in process. Specifically, we expect that publishing companies over the next decade will use communicating word processors to retrieve a manuscript stored in a computer composition facility by dialing that computer and calling for the file. The file might be displayed at the editor's screen or printed on a local high-speed printer and corrections and revisions could be made by the publishing house staff. Terminals capable of this sort of complex retrieval and editing are certain to be available by the mid 1980s. Bowne Time-Sharing recently announced the capability to interface remotely to several word processors, for example.

1.1.3   Classes of Equipment

Word processing equipment is offered in various configurations to support different total storage requirements and numbers of users. The first generation of equipment was introduced in 1964 by IBM with the announcement of the MT/ST (Magnetic Tape/Selectric Typewriter). In 1975, IBM introduced the MC/A or Magnetic Card Word Processor. Since then, a second generation of equipment distinguished by microcomputers and cathode ray tube input devices has been offered. The product classes are:

- *Stand-Alone Hard Copy*

    This equipment has limited editing and storage capability and usually employs hard-wired logic rather than microprocessors. It can be thought of as a bridge between typewriters and stand-alone display word processors. (See Figures 1.1.A, 1.1.B)

- *Stand-Alone Display*

    Display word processing equipment combines a standard keyboard and strike-on printer with a display device and, typically, two diskettes for text storage. Early devices of this type were produced by Vydec, Wang, Lexitron and Digital

FIGURE 1.1.A

STAND-ALONE NON-DISPLAY MEMORY TYPEWRITERS

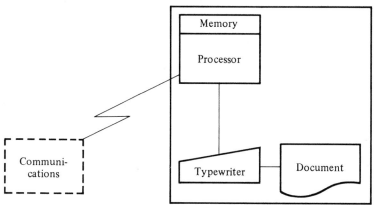

Hard wired or microprocessor
with software

– – – – – – – Optional

FIGURE 1.1.B

STAND-ALONE NON-DISPLAY

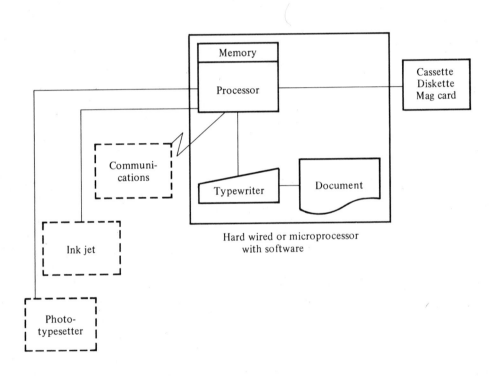

Hard wired or microprocessor
with software

– – – – – – – – Optional

Equipment. More recent equipment has been announced by Xerox and IBM. This equipment accommodates a single user, is based usually on diskettes (approximately 256,000 character storage) and is situated in the user's department.

Most of the equipment currently available uses a 15 inch diagonal cathode-ray tube to display the text — usually 24 lines of 80 characters each. Several efforts have been made to use a larger screen in a vertical mode to show the full contents of the standard 8½ by 11 inch page, although these efforts have in most cases produced smaller and less readable types. The Xerox 850, by contrast, uses high resolution cathode-ray tube capable of displaying black on white and constructing special characters — even type faces — on the face of the tube. We expect continued experimentation and progress to occur in this area. (See Figure 1.1.C).

Nearly all of the display word processors have used the daisy wheel printer design of Qume or Diablo. These printers typically operate at 55 characters per second and deliver letter-perfect quality with small incremental spacing capable of producing fully justified copy. In early 1978, Qume announced a printer with two printing heads, thus offering the operator an option of shifting quickly from one type face to another or adding complex mathematical and chemical characters to the normal typing font. A great deal of effort is now going on to find faster, low cost printers to be used in the office; ink jet printers and electrostatic printers are probable candidates. In our judgement, however, the strike-on printer sets the standard for quality that will have to be met by any machine used for formal correspondence or external reports.

Finally, display word processors normally have some communication capability. Most vendors today support both bi-synchronous and asynchronous protocols (i.e. IBM 2780, 3780 bi-synch and 2741 and TYY asynch).

The primary application of display word processors has been in multiple professional offices for the purpose of handling large reports, proposals, contracts and specifications. The equipment is excellent at making extensive revisions of long complex documents. A few machines — notably the Vydec machine — are quite good at handling financial and tabular data. The display word processors embody much better thinking in the area of keyboard layout and command structure and are therefore much easier to learn and to operate, but their high cost — $6,000 to $38,000 — continues to prevent most organisations from installing this equipment widely.

It is unlikely that the 50 or more present vendors of display word processing equipment will still be active in the market in five years. The cost of making pioneering sales of complex office equipment is too high to be carried by small firms for very long. Moreover, most users prefer to rent or lease the equipment during this period of constant technical change, putting an additional financial burden on the supplier. We believe that the equipment will become substantially better and expect continued introduction of high resolution displays.

Clustered

Realising the cost advantages per terminal by adding more terminals to the stand-alone microprocessor, these systems are expanded to accommodate usually two to four users. Each user can have a dedicated diskette yet share the central CPU and system software. These systems can also be located in the user department.

89

FIGURE 1.1.C

STAND-ALONE DISPLAY

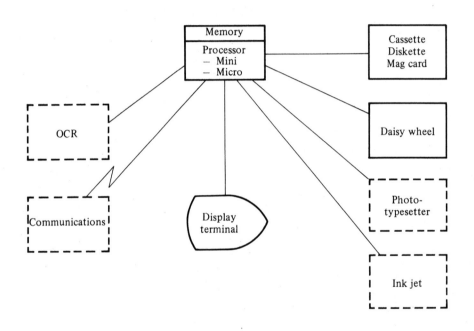

- - - - - Optional

- *Shared Logic*

    Mini-computer based, these systems can accommodate 32 or more users and incorporate large disk storage to be shared by all users. The system is centrally controlled and usually requires more investment in operator personnel, floor space, power, etc., as in a central DP environment. (See Figure 1.1.D).

- *Mainframe Based*

    Large mainframe manufacturers such as IBM, DEC, Honeywell and Univac offer software application packages that perform word processing functions. However, these packages are not as sophisticated as word processing systems (e.g. function key editing) and are not as cost effective above five or six terminals.

To interface to this class of system requires only a VDT. Usage is then billed on a monthly basis, directly proportional to time, degree and type of service provided.

This type of system service offers the user access to a large mainframe computing system at a minimal cost with centralised text storage for easy access from branch offices around the country. Data processing back-up and higher quality output, such as photocomposition output, are generally offered.

Charges are based on such parameters as minimum monthly charges, number of characters stored on-line and in archive storage, lines printed and connect-hours. A typical service, On-Line Systems Inc. of Pittsburgh, Pennsylvania has the following rates:

Monthly minimum charge	$5.00
On-line storage	5 cents/3.2K char/day
Archival storage	1 cent/3.2K char/day
Mounting charges (for tapes etc.)	$5.00
Line printer charge	5 cents/page

Other charges:

Charges for each hour connected	$10.00
Charges for computing time	5 cents/processor unit

1.1.4   Summary

The particular type of word processing equipment employed in any given office is dependent more upon how that equipment fits into the environment than upon equipment cost. For example, Figure 1.1.E shows that the cost per terminal is not significantly different between shared logic and clustered systems for systems with six or more terminals. When amortised over three years or more, there is little difference in cost per month per terminal, even for stand-alone equipment. Mainframe time-sharing is considerably more expensive (except for very low volumes of work) and does not offer the state-of-the-art software and function key terminals. Costs for this type of time-sharing service can run as high as $1,500 per month per terminal.

FIGURE 1.1.D

SHARED LOGIC

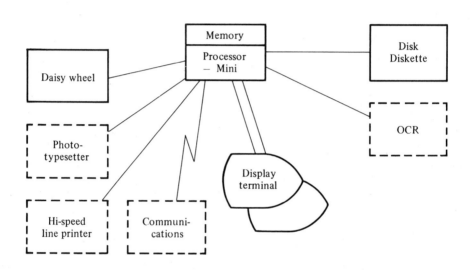

----- Optional

FIGURE 1.1.E

COMPARATIVE COSTS OF REPRESENTATIVE
WORD PROCESSING SYSTEMS

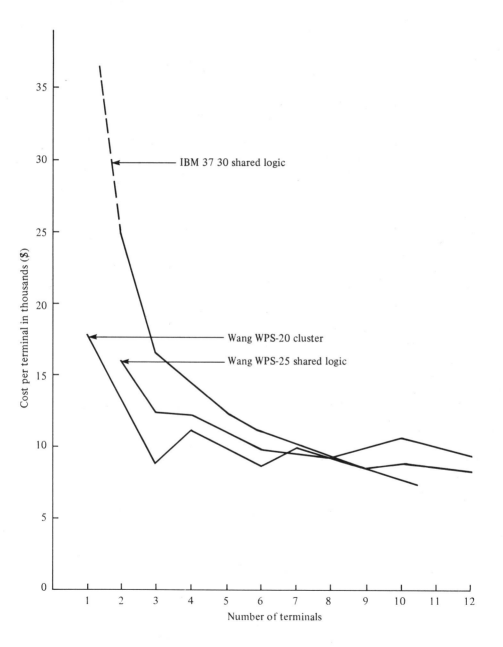

Table 1.1.A compares the capabilities of each class of system. Note that:

- Non-display equipment is not as powerful as display and appears to be more typewriter-like;

- The only difference between stand-alone display and shared logic is the capability to share common storage.

However, the stand-alone system is well suited to environments where autonomous operations are required and security is important. (See Table 1.1.B.)

Standards

Data are captured on disk or diskettes in either EBCDIC or ASCII format, which are universally recognised format codes. However, the structure of the disk on which the data are stored varies from one vendor to another, and so do the specialised format codes such as *centre* and *bold*.

However, almost all vendors recognise and support bi-synchronous or asynchronous communications protocols which allow the transfer of data to large mainframes.

Future

Migration toward a totally integrated office information system tying data processing, word processing, electronic mail, telecommunications and high quality production of materials is imminent. Existing word processors today will become intelligent work stations to a larger integrated system which will act as a message switcher and data base manager with store and forward capabilities. In addition, this message switcher will store information pertaining to the capabilities, location and load of the various output devices in the network (i.e. phototypesetters, intelligent copiers, line printers, ink jet devices, etc).

Current pioneering efforts are underway now by Wang with its OIS 100 series systems and IBM with its OS-6 series.

Suppliers

Typical vendors and products are listed in Table 1.1.C.

TABLE 1.1.A

COMPARISON OF WORD PROCESSORS

	Stand-alone non-display	Stand-alone display	Shared logic
Display	No	Yes	Yes
Editing	Light	Heavy	Heavy
Communications	No	Yes	Yes
Shared storage	No	No	Yes
Controller	Hard-wired or micro	Micro or mini	Micro AND mini
Output	Integral printer	Separate printer	Separate printer
1-Station cost	$2,000–$12,000	$6,000–$38,000	$12,000–$68,000

TABLE 1.1.B

FEATURES OF WORD PROCESSOR SYSTEMS

	Stand-alone	Stand-alone clustered (typically 1—4 term/cluster)	Shared logic (up to 30 + term/system)	Mainframe time-shared
Where located	User department	User department	Centrally (computer room)	MIS system
System operator	User	User	A designated system operator	MIS
Vendor coordination	A responsible group	A responsible group	A responsible group	MIS
On-going training	A responsible group/user	A responsible group/user	A responsible group/MIS	MIS
Security	Under user control	Under user control	Operator and user	MIS/User
Budget	Department	Department	Corporate	Corporate
Immediate exposure (Financial)	Low	Low	High	Low
Storage capability	Low (usually awkward)	Awkward (diskette)	Convenient (large disk)	Convenient (large disk)

TABLE 1.1.C

VENDORS OF WORD PROCESSING SYSTEMS

Stand-alone Non-display Memory Typewriters

Typical vendors:	IBM
	Exxon (QYX)
	Olivetti
Price range:	$2,000–$6,000

Stand-alone Non-display

Typical vendors:	Xerox
	IBM
	Exxon (QYX)
	Redactron
	CPT
Price range:	$4,000–$12,000

Stand-alone Display

Typical vendors:	Wang
	DEC
	Lanier
	IBM
	Exxon (Vydec)
Price range:	$6,000–$38,000

Shared Logic

		Maximum number stations supported:
Typical vendors:		
	Wang	24
	Four Phase	16
	DEC	48
	IBM	16
	Comtek	24
Entry cost range:	$12,000–$68,000	

1.2   Text Processing

1.2.1   History and Background

While we can find the earliest roots of automated composition in teletypesetter experiments during the late 1920s, the first substantive new technology appeared in 1948 when Harris Intertype developed the Photosetter. This modification of the mechanical linotype substituted a film negative for the recessed matrix and exposed the image of the character on photographic paper. Similar experiments undertaken by two French engineers resulted in a keyboard-operated phototypesetter which allowed the compositor to enter text at a typewriter-like keyboard while the machine spun a glass disk and flashed character after character onto photosensitive paper. The principal advantage of photocomposition was that the printer could go directly from a photographic image to an offset plate. The greatest disadvantage was the difficulty in correcting type once it had been imaged on a piece of paper. The compositor was required to cut out the incorrect line with a razor and paste in the correct version; sometimes it was necessary to reset the entire paragraph or page.

This problem of correction was the main puzzle during the early decade of automated composition systems and was the reason, in large part, for the development of text processing systems.

A computer was first programmed in 1961 to perform hyphenation and justification of text as well as insert a variety of typographic codes that would drive the phototypesetter on-line. This development made it possible to separate the keyboard activity from the phototypesetter. The idea was that several keyboard operators would punch "idiot" paper tape which was then hyphenated, justified and formatted by computer to drive a single phototypesetter. Speeds of 20 lines a minute, four times the rated linotype speed, were achieved.

Through the early 1960s, significant developments were made in phototypesetting technology that resulted in increased speed and greater typographic flexibility.

Stand-alone text processing terminals were developed which would read punched paper tape into a buffer and allow the editor to make corrections prior to repunching a new paper tape. By 1970, it was clear that this form of editing was essential to make phototypesetting a practical tool. The block and line mode of correction was abandoned in favour of interactive context-editing and the systems began to offer more sophisticated software including file management, search and alter, programmable keys and simple formatting.

Proofing and correction remained a major problem, however. In most systems, the only way to get a proof-perfect text was to set it on the phototypesetter, Xerox the output and make original corrections with a pencil. This practice was so costly in materials and labour that in many cases the new automated composition systems proved to be as expensive as the original hot metal line-casting systems and were often slower and less flexible.

During the same period, many users developed a variety of pagination strategies which attempted to assemble large blocks of text together in computer memory and thereby avoid the high cost of paste-up.

The switch from letter press to offset, beginning in the early 1950s and continuing today, led to several changes in platemaking technology. The most interesting current technology is laser platemaking which has the potential to image an offset plate directly from computer memory and thereby bypass composition entirely.

The major incentives for this last decade of technical innovation in publishing have included the opportunity for drastic cost reduction in the composition area by eliminating the need for the typesetter craftsmen. More recently, those who use the technology have begun to recognise the advantages of timely information handling and content control which are inherent in computer controlled composition systems. Newspapers were the first to experiment with automated composition; commercial printers have followed but their aim is to achieve substantial cost reductions and product improvements by going directly from a computer-managed data base to photo-typesetting.

The traditional method of composition (see Figure 1.2.A) provides a model for understanding the various automated composition technologies. Originally, the text was keyboarded at a linotype machine and stored in the form of metal slugs of "standing type". Proofs of this image were easily obtained by inking the type and printing one or two sheets. Proof readers compared the new image with the original manuscript and made corrections until a final clean proof was available for the author or editor. As large blocks of text were corrected, a compositor assembled them together as a page. When all pages had been made up, a single reproduction proof was made and photographed and this became the basis for offset platemaking.

Automated composition technologies have addressed each of these areas. In the new systems, text may be entered initially on a word processor and the diskette or cassette is then read into the text processing systems by way of an optical character recognition machine. Finally, in some complex systems such as newspapers, text entry is accomplished directly at an on-line terminal which shows the author the text as it will appear and allows him to make corrections as he works.

The text processing system stores the text in a data base form and performs a variety of processes including hyphenation and justification, file management, automatic formatting, sorting and pagination by algorithm.

The text can be proofed in two ways. It may be printed from computer memory on an available printer which will show the text and the typographic commands or it can be directed right to a phototypesetter which will show the final version of the type.

As before, the proof reader compares the original manuscript with the text and makes corrections until a clean proof is ready for the author. Large blocks of text are then pasted together to form a page in much the same way as hot metal is assembled in the make-up process.

FIGURE 1.2.A

TRADITIONAL AND AUTOMATED COMPOSITION PROCESSES

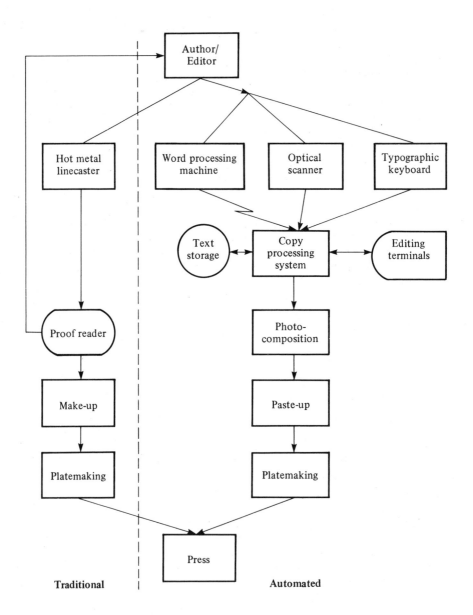

Traditional | Automated

SOURCE: Arthur D. Little, Inc.

100

From this brief introduction, it is clear that automated composition systems involve several technologies including word processing, optical character recognition, text processing systems, photocomposition, pagination and platemaking.

1.2.2   Text Processing Systems

Text processing systems differ from word processing systems primarily in their ability to manage very large data files. A text processing system may maintain thousands of pages of text. Although able to perform hyphenation and justification and support phototypesetting, in other respects text processing systems do much the same things as the latest word processors.

Text processing systems, like word processing systems, maintain a library of text stored on disks. Word processing software allows the operator to set tab stops, line length and page depth as well as to centre a line and set a paragraph with a ragged or justified right hand margin.

Text processing software also allows the operator to identify a type face, point size and leading to be used in the phototypesetter. It calculates the actual set size of the text and may assist the operator in fitting that block of text onto a page. Both classes of equipment are able to mark off a page of simple text, insert the appropriate page number and begin the next page with the right page header. When the operator inserts text or re-organises the content of the document, both the word processing system and the text processing system will repaginate the text automatically, change page numbers and re-organise the text. But neither word processors nor text editors have adequately dealt with the problems of breaking text into pages when the text contains tables or figures, and of fine pagination, following the stricter rules of formal composition.

Text processing systems cannot be operated in a normal office environment; they require a trained supervisor familiar with minicomputer hardware and software. They are used mainly in production shops associated with the development of complex documentation, specifications, catalogues and long formal reports.

The systems commercially available today have been designed largely as production tools and not for the management of large data bases; in our judgement, none of the current text processing systems employs what we know to be the best available data base management software. The latest and best of these systems organise their data files as a series of "stories" maintained in the author's queue.

Text processing systems will share with word processing systems any new developments in display technology, strike-on printing technology and keyboard layout.

1.2.3   Pagination

Pagination is the capability to create a typeset page, as a single "take" including all straight matter (body text), halftones, artwork, headings, rules, borders and folios positioned on a predetermined page in a particular order. The "take" is to be produced as a finished page on equipment compatible with the particular printing operation.

All of these functions can be performed individually using existing technology. For example, straight matter, headings and folios can be created with a typical text processing system; halftones, artwork and borders can be digitised and output to a CRT phototypesetter with the aid of a graphic digitiser; line rules can be drawn by a typcial CRT phototypesetter. The pagination dilemma is merging these functions on a common system that creates a single "take" automatically.

The laser plate maker offers the potential to eliminate the phototypesetter, film, chemicals, operators and paste-up by directly connecting to the text processing system. Since a plate cannot be cut and pasted as film, pagination is required.

The ink jet press, if developed, will eliminate the laser plate maker. Pages will be stored in digitised form in the computer and output to the ink jet press on the fly as the press runs at full speed. This technology has already been implemented in the computer industry by IBM and Mead Corporation for line printer applications.

All the equipment necessary to paginate exists today; the required development is in the software. However, not all the equipment can be purchased from a single vendor. Typically, the text processing system and the associated input and edit terminals are supplied to a newspaper as a package from a single vendor. The pitfalls were learned through the Newspapers Systems Development Group effort headed by IBM to develop the ultimate pagination system. Although the project failed, it did show the magnitude of the development effort required: the pagination process requires the consortium of multiple vendors leading to potential problems in identifying a single entity responsible for the system; pagination software has not been developed as a complete system; additional development is required on phototypesetters to merge text and graphics simultaneously; futhermore, laser plate-makers are new and not fully tested.

Pagination for the magazine and book industry is being implemented today. One total system is believed to cost approximately $1 million, much less than a newspaper system because the publication is smaller, requires fewer terminals and less storage, and tolerates longer response times because there is no daily edition.

In our opinion, pagination will be implemented within the next ten years. It is most probable that a large newspaper or chain will be the pioneer. Large scale complex systems are now under development by some of the larger newspapers including the Washington Post (using IBM, Raytheon and Data General equipment) and the Chicago Tribune (using DEC and Hendrix equipment). When pagination has been proven by the large newspapers and equipment costs are reduced, the smaller newspapers and other publishers will follow.

Standards

As in word processors, the data are captured on disks in ASCII format, since compatability with IBM EBCDIC format is of minimal use for most publishers. Disk structure and formatting commands vary from vendor to vendor.

The US Government Patent Office is attempting to adhere to a standard for typographical syntax commands. However, it is not universally recognised even in the USA.

1.3   Phototypesetting

Phototypesetting technology is stable and mature and products are best understood in three classes: *keyboard phototypesetters* such as the Addressograph Multigraph Compset 500 and the Compugraphic family of typesetters; medium-speed, *matrix photo-typesetters* such as Mergenthaler's VIP and the Dymo (Itek) Mark 3, 4 and 5; and the high-speed *cathode-ray tube phototypesetting equipment* such as the Autologic APS-5 and Information International's Videocomp.

The major difference between the last two categories is the difference in speed — 150 lines per minute versus 1,500 lines per minute, and cost — $25,000 versus $150,000. Small commercial printers have tended to buy two medium priced phototypesetters while composition intensive activities such as newspaper publishing, data base publishing and directory publishing use the very high-speed devices.

Keyboard phototypesetting, however, sets type only as fast as the user can operate the keyboard. More recent equipment provides the user with video display of the text and some of the same editing capabilities found in today's word processor. This ease of use combined with sharply reduced prices has meant that keyboard phototypesetting equipment can be brought into small publishing operations which had previously relied on strike-on typewriters or commercial composition.

One disadvantage shared by all phototypesetters is the chemical nature of the processing. Even keyboard phototypesetters are designed to expose photographic paper or film which must then be processed before it can be used. While the processing of this film is now done automatically by integrated film or paper processors, most phototypesetting installations still require extensive air conditioning and humidity control.

The economic advantage of full-page composition has induced vendors and users alike to continue experimenting with halftone composition and the composition of logos. Our review of the technology indicates that work in halftone composition is moving reasonably well. Information International Inc's 3300 halftone scanner employs a "titled diamond" dot structure which delivers an acceptable gray scale while taking reasonable advantage of computer logic. The photographs in US News and World Report are routinely imaged by this machine and while these photographs are admittedly coarse — usually an 85-line screen — the approach may work as well in finer resolutions of 110 lines per inch or higher. The composition of logos is not so much a technical problem as a question of economic storage.

Halftone composition has been viewed pessimistically by the newspaper community; the technology is not yet cost effective on their scale of operation. Nonetheless, several other users — notably International Graphics in Minneapolis — are able routinely to retrieve and "set" photographs with automated composition systems.

In the long term, phototypesetting may be displaced as a major part of an automated composition system by equipment which directly engraves a printing plate from computer memory. Well before that time, however, there must be developed an adequate high resolution proofing device which operates at low cost in materials. Xerographic printers offer one alternative for this; soft display pagination terminals offer another.

2. CONVERSION TECHNIQUES FOR EXISTING MATERIAL

2.1 Optical Character Recognition

2.1.1 Introduction

Optical scanning was one of the earliest methods tested for the initial keyboarding of text and since 1970 there have been several machines available to the graphic arts industry. Both CompuScan and ECRM developed OCR equipment capable of reading two or three typewriter faces and selling for $25,000 to $40,000 each. Since then, several smaller manufacturers such as Hendrix, Context, Xicon and others have developed smaller and faster OCR devices capable of reading two to three pages per minute of a normal double-spaced typed manuscript.

Current OCR technology reads the characters on a page by scanning the page with a laser beam, recording the occurrence of black and translating that occurrence into patterns. These patterns are compared to other patterns stored in the scanner's "library" and those which are recognised are translated into 8-bit code for that character used by computers. Characters which cannot be recognised may be flashed on an associated editing terminal where the operator can make a judgement. Alternatively, some systems attempt to guess what the character is and rely on the proof reader to verify the guess.

Several efforts have been made to build very large optical scanners capable of reading virtually any typeset font – such equipment was built by Recognition Equipment Corporation, by CompuScan and by Information International. These machines, costing in excess of $1 million, are not now commercially available. Other equipment developed principally by the Japanese is capable of reading handwritten numerals and hand printed letters. That technology has been applied primarily to the recognition of banking and business documents.

Several developments are expected in the area of OCR. We look forward to remote scanners costing less than $8,000 which will scan a document and transmit the unrecognised bit stream via a communications network to a host processor – possibly the existing mainframe computer – where character recognition will take place. In another development, hybrid OCR/facsimile is expected to become available in the United States within the next few years. Such equipment will recognise as many characters as it can at the local OCR station, and when it encounters material that cannot be recognised – signatures, photographs and drawings – it will transmit this material in facsimile mode.

Thus, the information stream from the scanner will be a mixture of byte-oriented character information and bit-oriented image information which is reconstructed at the distant end.

One of the obstacles to widespread use of optical character recognition has been the amount of coding effort imposed on the original typist. This can be largely eliminated in the current OCR equipment through proper programming.

2.1.2   Existing Scanning Technologies

2.1.2.1   Character Scanning

As outlined, there are various OCR products available today that scan pre-formatted, typewritten copy in the context of generating new material. However, there are only a few products available on the market that can scan and read printed material such as books, newspapers, etc.

There are two vendors recognised today as leaders and pioneers in this area, (III and Kurtzweil). III entered the market by designing a special scanner for the Jacksonville Air Rework Facility to digitise existing repair/parts manuals and store in a data base for updating and regeneration. The system uses a DEC KA-10 CPU and is capable of scanning, digitising and storing multiple fonts at a speed of approximately 1,000 characters/second. The system sells for about $3 million. Error rates are quoted to be less than one per cent. Only one other system was sold, to the Department of Health & Social Security in Great Britain.

The input media must be 35 MM negatives. Particular fonts to be recognised must be pre-scanned into the system and are denoted at the time of scanning by means of an electronic tablet or light pen.

A slower, less expensive OCR that reads multi fonts is offered by Kurtzweil Computer Products, Inc. At a rated speed of 30 characters/second and a quoted error rate of 1/20,000 characters, the KDEM (Kurtzweil Data Entry Machine) was originally developed as a reading aid for the blind. The KDEM reads source documents in their original form including hardcover and softcover books, magazines, newspapers, etc.

Although the KDEM has "a priori" knowledge of character shapes and will put its best guess for any alphanumeric character on a display screen, a brief training period is generally required to refine its knowledge of fonts before the machine can be put into production mode to run unattended. A system composed of a CRT (per operator control), scanner disk drive and tape drive costs upwards of $100,000.

All existing OCR's consist of six basic elements: feeder/transport unit, scanner, recognition unit, controller, output stacker, and data output units.

The transport unit moves the forms from the input hopper past the scanner to the output stacker. The type of transport used at the reading station is largely dependent on the scanning method. If the scanner is fixed, the paper must move; but if the paper proceeds at a fixed rate, the scanner must move.

The scanner converts the printed character to electrical signals for analysis by the recognition unit. Optical scanning is based on contrast differences between the characters and their background. Table 2.1.A shows the various types of scanners.

The recognition unit (both hardware and software controlled) interprets the characters. Table 2.1.B outlines the various types of units offered today.

TABLE 2.1.A

SCANNER TYPES

Mechanical disk	Low cost, slow
Flying spot	High cost, flexible, limited resolution
Laser	High resolution, slow
Parallel photocells	High cost, fast, inflexible
Vidicon (TV projection)	No document movement, slow

TABLE 2.1.B

RECOGNITION METHODS

Optical matching	Simple, cheap, error prone
Matrix matching	Fast, flexible, cheap
Stroke analysis	Slow
Feature detection	Slow, expensive, multi-font
Curve tracing	Reads hand printing

2.1.2.2 Illustration Scanning

This type of scanning requires more than deciphering black tones from white tones. Analogue signals represent different gray levels – i.e. varying degrees of light – by analogous levels of electrical intensity.

In order to transfer ink from print to paper, a screening process must be used. The screening process transforms the continuous tone image into a series of "dots" or "cells". The nature and size of cells will be determined by the kind of screen used. It is not necessary to screen type or line unless there are very heavy solids, in which case a screen or screen effect is often used which might vary from perhaps five-ten per cent to 90-95 per cent to convey the effect of a light gray shading or a solid.

Any picture, photograph, or scene consisting of a broad range of tones or graduation of tones is known as continuous tone.

In letterpress and offset lithography, tones cannot be reproduced by varying the amounts of ink. A press can print only a solid of a colour in image areas, while no ink prints in the non-image areas. In order to produce pictures in varying tones, graphic art photography uses a halftone screen. Halftone photography makes printing of continuous-tone photographs possible by converting continuous-tone image into a pattern of very small and clearly defined dots of varying sizes. The halftone principle is an optical illustion in which tones are represented by a large number of small dots of different sizes printed with ink of uniform film thickness.

Thus, in scanning a photograph for reproduction (by means of "typesetting" directly onto film for plate making or directly onto a printing plate),some method of screening the picture electronically must be contrived, unless scanning an image that has already been screened. However, the latter process eliminates the possibility of subsequent sizing (screening resolution would have to be changed). Also, quality may suffer since one dot pattern would be interposed onto another.

Aside from the matter of resolution (usually 25 to 50 per cent for printing) there is a problem of gray scale. For example, a 256 gray level requirement would require 8 bits description for each level. Other methods, such as contours to represent gray level values, are being investigated.

Typical systems such as the III 3600 Scanner are approved today. The Associated Press transmits halftones electronically via its "electronic darkroom" process recently developed.

2.1.2.3 Colour

Electronic scanning can be used to produce the equivalent of colour separation by photographic masking. A light beam scanning the original is split into three beams. Each beam goes to a photocell covered with a filter that corresponds to one of the three primary colours: blue, red or green (these three colours when added together produce white light).

2.1.3 Summary

We have outlined various optical character readers and image scanners offered on the market today. In summary, we can emphatically state that the capability to digitise, store and output text, line-out, and halftones (including colour) is state-of-the-art. However, the total storage required to store and format a mixture of data (characters and image) is astronomical and not cost effective for most applications. More development in the areas of data compression and storage device costs is required. For quality output, gray level definition research is required.

2.1.4 Suppliers of OCR Equipment

ADL identified a representative sample but did not compile a comprehensive directory of suppliers of multifont equipment in the course of its survey of OCR technology.

Vendor	Product	Address
CompuScan Inc.	Alphawood	900 Huyler Street Teterboro New Jersey 07608
Formscan (agent)	Alphawood	Apex House West End Frome Somerset BA11 3AS
Kurzweil	KDEM	264 Third Street Cambridge Massachusetts 02142
Telesensory Systems Inc.	Optacon	3408 Hillview Avenue P O Box 10099 Palo Alto California 94304
Information International Inc.	Grafix 1	5933 Slansen Avenue Culver City California 90230
Recognition Equipment Inc.	Input 80	P O Box 22307 Dallas Texas 75222

Vendor	Product	Address
Scan-data Corp.	2250-1	800 East Main Street Norristown Pennsylvania 19401
Scan-optics Inc.	501	22 Prestige Park Road East Hartford Connecticut 06108

2.2   Facsimile

2.2.1   Types of Equipment

Description

Facsimile equipment relays alphanumeric and graphic data to remote sets through telephone or transmission lines, or via radio and microwave communication links. The original document is scanned, converted into electrical signals and transmitted to a remote site where a copy is made.

Classes of Equipment

Three classes of facsimile machines have been defined by CCITT:

- Class 1 (4—6 minutes FM) for A4 page (agreed 1975);
- Class 2 (2—3 minutes AM) for A4 page (agreed 1976);
- Class 3 (less than 1 minute digital) for an A4 page (agreed 1978).

Installed Base

The vast majority of the installed base is represented by Class 1 terminals while Group 2 and Group 3 represent one quarter of the total. However, Group 2 and Group 3 terminals are going to conquer large parts of the market. By 1985, Group 2 and Group 3 terminals will represent the majority of the European installed base.

Categories of Equipment

There are three major categories of fax equipment (Figure 2.2.A):

- Business convenience machines;
- High speed "operation" machines;
- Special purpose equipment.

Convenience machines are simple but generally offer a poor service (poor resolution, low operating speed, manual loading). However, they do enable their user to deliver a few pages to the corresponding fax machine quickly. They are built to handle few copies per day. A low cost machine pays the penalty of having relatively long transmission times: six minutes.

The convenience machines today are in fact Class 1 machines, but the Class 2 standard is also for convenience machines. The usual transmission medium for such machines is the telephone line. The Class 3 standard may be used in the convenience machine market.

113

FIGURE 2.2.A
FACSIMILE TERMINALS BY USE AND TYPE

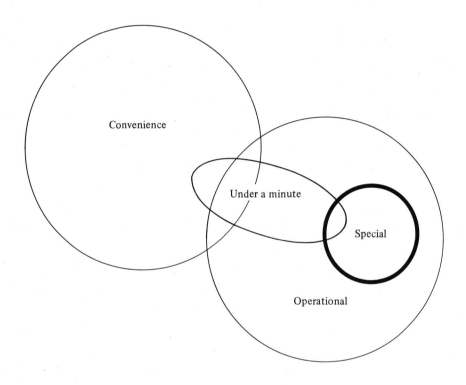

Convenience

Under a minute

Special

Operational

SOURCE: Arthur D. Little, Inc.

114

Operational facsimile machines are intended to handle more copies per day than the convenience machine. They are regarded as heavy-duty backroom devices which provide a rudimentary form of inter-office electronic mail.

The transmission speed is one minute or less per page and the standard followed is Class 3. Such machines are often attached to the company network or special public networks rather than to the telephone line.

Within the operational facsimile machines class, there are some special fax machines for news wire-photo services, weather information and for printing and publishing applications.

These machines operate at high speed: 72 Kbps or higher.

2.2.2   Technology

Convenience Equipment

A typical convenience device is represented in Figure 2.2.B. The transmitter includes a scanner, usually a rotating drum and an illuminating and photosensitive pick-up means. The machine gathers information on the density of the document in small areas by scanning the copy in a regular and repetitive pattern. Timing signals are added to the electrical data signals thus generated and a composite stream of analogue data is transmitted over the dial-up telephone system.

At the receiving end, the process is reversed. The receiver is locked into synchronism with the transmitter in terms of both speed and phase angle. The incoming data signal causes the receiving machine to mark on its rotating receiving sheet (burn-off paper) a series of picture elements corresponding exactly in location and intensity to those picked up by the transmitter. Much of the hardware for both scanning and receiving is shared in order to cut the cost of the equipment. In the most inexpensive units, synchronisation is accomplished by locking into the power line frequency rather than by maintaining two internal synchronised time standards. More expensive models offer various automatic or unattended operating models as extra-cost options.

Operational Equipment

The high-capacity and under-a-minute operational machines have a significantly different architecture. In addition to the scanners and printing mechanisms found in convenience units, the operational machines utilise a modem rather than a modulator, and some form of data compressor/re-constructor. The typical structure of the operational machines is shown schematically in Figure 2.2.C.

The scanner, most often faster than those used in simple convenience machines, generates a data stream and synchronises information – usually in digital rather than analogue form. The stream of digits generated represents strings of black and white picture elements. The data stream is

FIGURE 2.2.B

SIMPLE SYNCHRONOUS SYSTEM AS USED IN CONVENIENCE FACSIMILE MACHINES

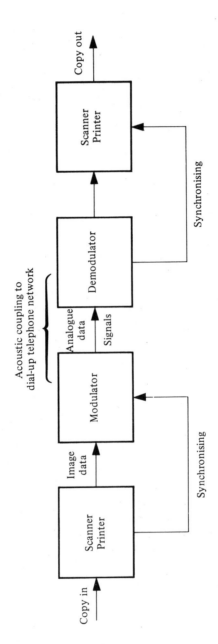

SOURCE: Arthur D. Little

116

FIGURE 2.2.C

COMPLEX ASYNCHRONOUS DIGITAL SYSTEM AS USED IN HIGH-SPEED FACSIMILE MACHINES

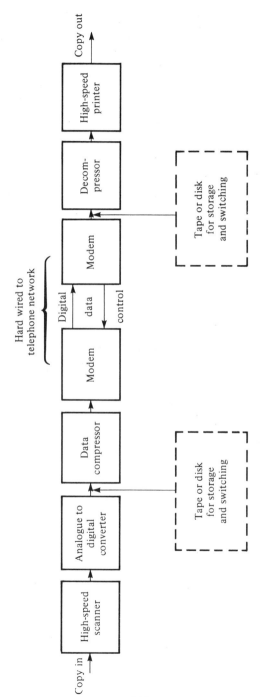

SOURCE: Arthur D. Little

117

arithmetically and logically processed by the data compressor to remove redundant data, thereby producing a short, "enriched" bit stream. The compressed data, similar to computer data, are fed to the modem which generates signals best adapted to maximise the transmission rate over the interconnecting link.

In some circumstances, it will retransmit data blocks, if, by return channel, it detects that the receiving system has received errors. The modem at the receiving end receives the stream of compressed data bits, expands them by inverse arithmetic computation and reproduces the image on one of several forms of high-speed printer. The combination of data compression and recon-struction and the use of a sophisticated modem able to maximise data throughput over the transmission line enables the high-resolution fast fax systems to operate over low-capacity circuits.

Unlike the simpler convenience machines which rely on synchronous operating systems, the high speed operational units operate in uneven patterns: they start and stop as data and processing rates vary and as buffers fill and empty. Actual per-page transmission times vary depending upon the complexity of the image sent and the time required to perform the data compression and decompression. Many operational machines include mechanisms which allow unattended oper-ation.

The costs of the equipment reflect these capabilities. Such costs can reasonably be borne on a per-page basis only by users with heavy-use applications and only because transmission line-costs can be saved by using data compression and fast modems.

There is little common ground between simple manual convenience machines and the high-speed class. To provide speeds of much less than two minutes/page, resolution (quality of image) is sacrificed if cost constraints require that simple equipment be built. If speeds of under a minute are needed, the compressor, the modem, the high-speed scanner and the high-speed printer are all required and a three- or four-fold increase in cost (and efficiency) results.

2.2.3 Typical Prices

A convenience fax will sell today for around $1,500 if it uses the Class 1 standard. A conveni-ence fax using Class 2 standard will be sold for around $2,500. An operational fax will be sold for around $12,000.

Typical examples:

Xerox 400 (4 or 6 minutes), half duplex, manual feed	around $1,500 rent around $50 per month
Xerox 410 (4 or 6 minutes), half duplex automatic feed	around $4,000 rent around $120 per month

118

Panafax MV1200 (4 minutes), duplex	rent around $80 per month
Xerox 485 (Fuji 490) (1 minute) automatic feed, automatic and unattended	around $7,000

2.2.4   Main Manufacturers Selling in Europe Today

Kalle Infotec, Siemens, CIT-Alcatel, Muirhead, Plessey/3M, Xerox.

2.2.5   Performance and Range of Application

The convenience fax (Class 1) will be used within small offices or on the desks of secretaries. It is used for transmitting a few copies per day — typically two to five. It is attached to the telephone network and typical bit rate is 1,200 bps or 2,400 bps.

The convenience fax (Class 2) will find the same use as the Class 1 fax. It will typically transmit say five to ten copies per day.

The operational fax will be used as a heavy-duty backroom device. This fax will be typically attached to a leased line at 4.8 or 9.6 Kbps. The total cost involved in running such a fax machine — i.e. its price and the lease of a voice grade channel — requires significant use of the machine: typical figures would be a few dozen copies per day. The special fax, by definition, requires a special and heavy usage.

2.2.6   Expected and Possible Developments in the Next Decade

The forcing factors will be the progress of electronics. It is expected that the price of processing a block of data will decrease faster than the price of transmitting it. Therefore effort will be made by manufacturers to improve fax redundancy coding techniques to have a convenience fax able to transmit one page in less than one minute by 1985–1987.

The high probability scenario runs as follows:

The Class 3 fax is going to be dominant in the mid 1980s. Its price will decrease to around $5,000.

The operational fax will have more capabilities. It is expected that some fax equipment will be connected to main memory systems to enable them to use a fax switch shared by more than one user. The corresponding sets could be located close to the end user.

Another version would be an upgrade of the smart copier (the IBM 6670) which would include the fax transmission/reception capabilities. The price today would be in the range of 40K to 80K dollars.

119

The low probability scenario would show the fax machine signal processing capabilities remaining as they are with a slightly declining price, say three per cent per year.

2.2.7   Comments

Facsimile machines can work on a packet switched network. Fax-Pack from ITT enables non-compatible fax terminals to communicate via a packet switched network which translates between the two fax terminals. The translation is performed for Class 1 terminals.

Compression Labs has built a facsimile machine controller called Fax Comp. A Fax Comp unit can send or receive from CCITT Group 1, 2 and 3 machines as well as from ASCII or Baudot terminals. Fax Comp is priced at $3,900, and can be tied to a computer which then can become a network node. Such a node can support 28 Fax Comps.

Compression Lab has also developed a facsimile answering machine which can receive a fax image while unattended. This machine, "Fax-mate", acts as a store and forward buffer and costs $600.

The French PTT plan to put on the market a simple convenience facsimile costing around $500 within two to three years.

2.2.8   Suppliers of Facsimile Equipment

ADL identified a representative sample, but did not compile a comprehensive directory of suppliers of Group 3 and similar digital facsimile equipment in the course of its survey of the technology.

Vendor	Product	Address
AM International Inc.	Communicating Copier	1900 Avenue of the Stars Los Angeles California 90067
Graphic Sciences Inc.	Dex 5100	Corporate Drive Commerce Park Danbury Connecticut 06810
3M	Express 9600	Business Communications Product Group P O Box 1 Bracknell Berkshire, England

Vendor	Product	Address
Ricoh Company	Rapifax Systems 50	Rapicon Inc. 7 Kingsbridge Road Fairfield New Jersey 07006
Muirhead	K3000	Muirhead Data Communications Limited 34 Croydon Road Beckenham Kent BR3 4BE
Plessey	UF20, UF320	Plessey Telecommunications Limited Justin Manor 341 London Road Mitcham Surrey
Matsushita Electric Industrial Company (Japan) Visual Sciences Inc	Panafax UF20	900 Whitman Road Huntingdon Station New York 11746
Kalle Infotec	Infotec 6000 (Rapifax)	Hobson House 155 Gower Street London WC1E 6BJ
CIT Alcatel	Citedex	33 Rue Emerian 75725 Paris Cedex 15
Philips	P-Fax 2003	Philips Telecommunications P O Box 32 1200 JD Hilversum The Netherlands
Compression Labs Inc.	Faxcomp	10440 Tantass Avenue Cupertino California

2.2.9   Facsimile Networks

Southern Pacific Communications	SPEED-FAX
ITT Domestic Transmission Systems Inc. New York	FAX-PAK
Graphic Scanning Corp	GRAPHNET
RCA Global Communications Inc.	Q-FAX
US Postal Service / British Post Office Corporation	INTELPOST
British Post Office Corporation	MUFAX
Deutsche Bundespost	TELEFAX
French PTT	TELEFAX
Japanese KDD	QUICK FAX
Cable and Wireless Limited	BUREAUFAX

3. ARCHIVAL STORAGE DEVICES

3.1 Introduction

The purpose of this investigation was to identify those technologies which show the greatest promise for storing a large number of documents in an on-line, electronically accessible form at a reasonable cost during the mid to late 1980s. We have assumed that in order to be useful for the intended application, the system must have, at a minimum, the following characteristics:

- Average access time of less than 60 seconds with no human intervention required subsequent to mounting the archive;

- Total system storage capacity of at least 1×10^{12} characters (10 terabits);

- Non-volatile, permanent storage capability, such that an intentional action must be taken to erase or modify the stored data.

As might be expected, all such storage devices fall into the category of archival storage devices as defined in common data processing usage. In the past, such devices have always been used as a part of a storage hierarchy. This storage hierarchy contained at least one other type of storage device which had smaller capacity and faster average access time. Over the past several years, these storage hierarchy systems have become more complex in that they have involved one or more intelligent controllers and at least three levels of storage devices (including the main storage of the data processing equipment).

Within the next five years, we believe that this storage hierarchy concept will be extended to contain three levels of mass storage. The slower two levels will remain similar to those found today — i.e. they will consist of moving head disks, and some type of semi-random access, optical or magnetic technology-based mass storage device. The third (fastest) level will consist of a relatively small amount (one to four million bytes) of fast, block-oriented random access storage devices utilising CCD or magnetic bubble technology.

This third level of mass storage has the same effect on average access time as do the "cache" memories in the main storage systems in the mainframe. In the mass storage systems, these caches are expected to improve average access times by at least a factor of 2.5 — i.e. these times are expected to range from two to 15 milliseconds compared with the current 30 to 50 milliseconds for moving head disks.

It is believed that these caches will also come under the control of the intelligent storage controller as in the current IBM 3850 mass storage systems. Thus, the entire storage hierarchy would operate in parallel with the mainframe with all inter-level data transfers, error recovery, alternate track assignment, and other physical media-related functions being handled by the controller.

It is our opinion that all of the archival storage devices discussed below will be part of such a storage hierarchy in actual use. Many factors went into the formation of this opinion which involve such system constraints as storage and utilisation of industries, device accessing characteristics, and the use of required fall-back and recovery mechanisms. However, there is one overriding consideration which, in our opinion, makes the use of such a hierarchical storage system necessary. That consideration stems from the difference in bandwidth between the mass storage device and the communications and/or hard copy device used to transmit the data to and from the document storage centres. In almost all conceivable cases, there would be a sufficiently large difference in the bandwidths between these two types of devices to make it inappropriate to transmit the data from the archival storage device directly through the output device without some, and probably a relatively large amount of, buffer storage. Storage hierarchy systems inherently have this buffering capability and in many cases, it is as important a characteristic of the hierarchy as is the decrease in average access time provided by using multiple levels of storage.

Therefore, in the description which follows of the various archival storage technologies which would be utilised, we have made the implicit assumption that each of these types of devices would be utilised as part of a larger storage hierarchy system. The non-archival storage levels of the hierarchy would make use of bubble, CCD, or MOS RAM for the faster level and moving head sealed disks for the slower level. These technologies would not be considered for the archival level. Since the size and access characteristics of the other levels of the storage hierarchy are not strongly dependent upon the characteristics of the archival storage device, it is our opinion that the cost of the surrounding storage hierarchy and processing system will be invariant with the type of archival system actually used and hence will not become a factor in determining the choice of the appropriate technology for the archival system.

3.2   Technology Review

There are four major technologies which we believe have a reasonable probability of being developed for use as on-line archival storage systems:

1.   Mass storage systems — These include magnetic tape, magnetic cartridge and video tape systems. Such media are erasable, unlike other alternatives. They are commercially available from IBM, CDC, CalComp and SDC/AMPEX.

2.   Optical mass storage — These laser-written/light-read strips coated with metal are compact and do not deteriorate over time. The Precision Instruments Company offers two such products. As archival storage, their read-only property is acceptable, if not an advantage. Techniques for placing strips in cartridges, à la magnetic tape, and selecting a cartridge will enhance capacity and random access.

3.   Optical video disk — These laser-written/light-read disks are durable, rugged and portable. They are read-only. One has recently been announced by Toshiba. Philips Labs is the US leader in research. Techniques for storing multiple disks and selecting a disk as in a juke box, will enhance capacity.

4.   Holographic memories — These are created by creating two- or three-dimensional diffraction patterns of the data. Holography has the greatest potential for rapid access. Many engineering problems remain to be solved, especially in mechanical support for reading and writing. They are currently read-only. The Harris Corporation has installed one system which uses encoded microfiche as a base. Among those pursuing this technology are Bell Labs, IBM, RCA, Siemens, Nippon, Hitachi and Thomson-CSF.

We also studied microform for archival storage use. Except as a part of certain holographic memory systems, microform is suitable only for off-line, backup storage. Furthermore, as an analogue medium, it is strictly an input medium to a document digitalisation system like ARTEMIS.

Mass storage technology devices (tape and video) have been in use in the field for several years and are likely to be competitive for a long time. There is opportunity for capacity and cost improvements, especially if several vendors continue to support these devices. The optical technologies are just emerging from the laboratory into the marketplace; it will take time to reach their full potential. Table 3.2.A summarises critical parameters of each technology. Where possible, these values reflect commercial products available today; otherwise estimates are provided. It is clear that optical video disks and holographic memories potentially have far superior access times.

Figure 3.2.A presents estimates of the maximum capacity of each technology versus time. The slopes of the lines represent the rate of maturity and improved density of each technology. This rate of progress depends to a large extent on the level of demand for each system. Mass storage systems will remain competitive with all optical mass memory for the next decade. If optical mass memory matures at the rate estimated, it will provide the greatest capacity soonest.

TABLE 3.2.A

MASS STORAGE TECHNOLOGY

Memory technology	Typical capacity	Access time	Cost
Video and tape mass storage systems	1.1 terabits	7 to 15 seconds	29 to 190 microcents/bit
Optical mass storage	1.0 terabits	7 to 20 seconds	360 microcents/bit
Optical video disk	0.01* terabits	7.5 seconds (future — less than one second)	Up to 20* microcents/bit
Holographic memories	0.2* terabits	Less than 15 seconds (future in millisecond range)	2.5* microcents/bit for the media

*Estimates of current devices

FIGURE 3.2.A
CAPACITY VS. TIME

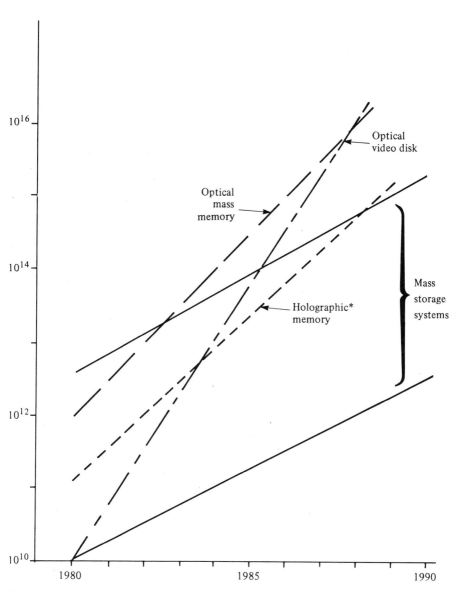

10^{16}

Optical
video disk

Optical
mass
memory

10^{14}

Mass
storage
systems

Holographic*
memory

10^{12}

10^{10}

1980   1985   1990

*Commercial products may be available circa 1984
SOURCE: ADL estimates

Figure 3.2.B presents estimated archival memory costs in cents per bit versus time. In these figures, we have tried to include the cost of mechanical components — e.g. for reading, writing and unit selection as well as media costs. In most cases, the media costs fall far more rapidly than those of the mechanical portions. Costs represent prices paid by the commercial customers, when devices are or become available. Optical technologies may become economical in the near future.

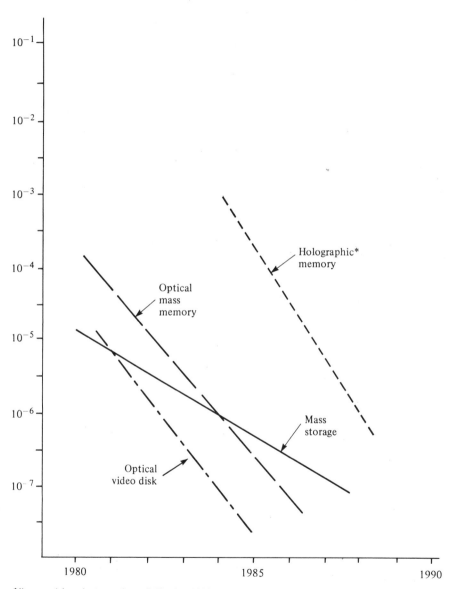

FIGURE 3.2.B

COST VS. TIME

Holographic* memory

Optical mass memory

Mass storage

Optical video disk

*Commercial products may be available circa 1984

3.3   Recommendations

In the near term (now until 1984), mass storage systems will be the only devices available which provide the necessary capacity for large archival storage systems. Optical mass memories will exceed terabit capacities and will become cost competitive with mass storage about 1984. Optical video disks will reach terabit capacities about that time; costs may be significantly lower than either form of mass storage.

Both optical mass memories and optical video disks should be competitive alternatives to tape and video mass storage beyond 1984. Cost/capacity/access-time/space requirements should determine the preferred approach.

Holographic memories have the furthest to go before reaching terabit capacities. Cost of the total device, media and delivery system may never be competitive with other approaches.

Choice of archival storage technology depends upon the time frame for implementation. Before 1984, one should select from among available mass (tape or video) storage systems. The preferred vendor will depend on the parameters of individual systems. If implementation occurs after 1984, optical mass memory and optical video disks would be considered.

Because archival storage is only one level of the computer memory hierarchy, the rest of the system is independent of the archival storage technology used. Several scenarios are possible:

1.   Implement all systems, starting before 1984, using mass storage.

2.   Implement early systems with mass storage and later ones with optical devices.

3.   Implement systems with mass storage and replace with optical devices when they become cost effective.

3.4   Suppliers of Archival Storage Systems

ADL identified a representative sample, but did not compile a comprehensive directory of suppliers of archival mass storage systems in the course of its survey of memory technology.

Vendor	Product	Address
CalComp	7110	California Computer Products Inc. 2411 W la Palma Avenue Anaheim CA 92801
Control Data Corp.	38500	Box "O" Minneapolis Minnesota 55440
IBM Corp.	3850	Data Processing Division 1133 Westchester Avenue White Plains New York 10604
SDC/Ampex Corp.	TBM	1020 Kifer Road Sunnyvale California 94086
Precision Instruments Corp.	Unicon 690 Unicon 190	Santa Clara California
Toshiba Corp.	(prototype Videodisc)	1-6 Uchisaiwai-cho 1-Chome Chiyoda-ku Toyko, Japan
Philips Laboratories	(prototype Videodisc)	Briarcliff Manor New York 10510
International Video Corp.	IVC-1000	453 West Maude Avenue Sunnyvale California 94086

REFERENCES

ADL 78   "Study of Future Computer Technology, Market, and Environment", ADL (Japan), December 1978, p. 1–15, 1–16, 1–36, 1–37, 1–38.

DATA 77,   "Control Data 38500 Mass Storage System", DATAPRO,
70D–263   Datapro Research Corporation, Delran, N.J., September 1977, p. 70D–263–21a–21d.

DATA 78,   "CalComp 7110 Automated Tape Library", DATAPRO, Datapro
70D–118   Research Corporation, Delran, N.J., April 1978, p. 70D–118– 01a–01c.

GILl 75   Gillis, A. K. et al, "Holographic Memories – Fantasy or Reality", National Computer Conference, 1975, p. 535–539.

GRAV 78   Graves, C. M., "National Westminster Bank Mass Storage Archiving", *IBM Systems Journal,* Vol. 17 No. 4, 1978, p. 344–358.

HOAG 79   Hoagland, A. S., "Storage Technology: Capabilities and Limitations", COMPCON, Spring 1979, IEEE, p. 60–64.

JOHN 75   Johnson, C., "IBM 3850 – Mass Storage System", National Computer Conference, 1975, p. 509–514.

KACZ 77   Kaczorowski, E. M., "Optical Mass Storage", COMPCON, Spring 1977, IEEE, p. 33–36.

KENN 77   Kenny, G., et al, "An Optical Disc Data Recorder", COMPCON, Spring 1977, IEEE, p. 31–32.

LASE 77   "Laser-Powered Data Bank Developed by Toshiba", *The Japan Times,* September 13, 1977, p. 7.

LEMM 77   Lemmond, C. Q., et al, "Advanced Archival Memory", General Electric Corporate Research and Development, Schenectady, N.Y., April 1977, AD–A067 567.

NELS 76   Nelson, R. H., "High Capacity Optical Data Storage and Retrieval Systems", International Telemetering Conference 1976, p. 348–355.

REYN 77   Reynolds, G., "Optical/Holographic Memories", internal ADL memorandum, February 2, 1977.

SCHN 75   Schneidewind, N., et al, "Mass Memory System Peripherals",
           COMPCON, 1974, IEEE, p. 87–91.

THEI 78   Theis, D. J., "An Overview of Memory Technologies", *Datamation*,
           Janaury 1978, p. 113–130.

WARN 79   Warner, B. J., et al, *Computer Science and Technology: Computer
           Peripheral Memory System Forecast*, NBS Special Publication 500–45,
           U.S. Department of Commerce, April 1979.

4.   STORAGE FOR THE END USER AND FOR DATA EXCHANGE

4.1   Requirements of ARTEMIS

In most terminal systems, some method of storage is needed. The basic function of the memory subsystem is to decouple the distribution network from the display devices and the user. This can take the form of a small buffer memory to permit burst transmission and a slower, constant-rate output.

Since many of these memory devices are small, cheap and demountable, they can also be used as information transfer devices between low volume input or output operations and the large archival stores. They are generally rugged enough to go through the mail or be delivered by messenger.

The capacity requirements for the storage system are dictated by the modes of transmission and display, as well as by the content and format of the information. Buffer storage capacity would range from a page, say, 15,000 bits to 500,000 bits to store a fax image.

There is a dramatic difference in storage capacity requirements between coded text and facsimile presentations. The latter might pose a serious cost burden if multiple-image storage were desired. One solution to this problem is the use of data compression, which not only increases storage efficiency but also allows faster transmission over bandwidth-limited networks. Several techniques have been developed for reducing the number of bits needed to represent a fax image; data reduction factors ranging from five to ten have been achieved, depending on the characteristics of the image. These systems, which exploit the statistics of typical images and utilise sophisticated encoding techniques, would be simple to implement at the transmitter. (See Appendix 7).

4.2 Technical Options

4.2.1 Semiconductor Memory

Because of their small size per memory bit, high speed and low manufacturing cost, semi-conductor memories are now used in data processing, mini- and microcomputers to the exclusion of almost all others.

The newer semiconductor devices can provide 16,000 to 65,000 bits of storage on one chip, so that for many small-scale applications such as terminals and minicomputers the requisite amount of main memory can be obtained with just a few devices.

Since each semiconductor memory device now is essentially a small, self-contained memory system, memory capability can be physically distributed throughout the computing system wherever needed for architectural considerations with little cost penalty.

4.2.2 Charge Coupled Devices (CCD)

Unlike conventional semiconducting devices, which provide random access memory, charge coupled devices provide serial access information storage, and are therefore functionally analogous to magnetic tape or disk storage. In a CCD, information bits are stored as packets of electrical charge distributed along a chain of semiconducting registers on a silicon chip; by shifting these packets along the chain under electronic control, the desired bit can be accessed at the output end. The potential storage density of the CCD per chip is estimated to be three to four times greater than that of dynamic MOS RAM. Another use for CCDs is the direct storage and read-out of images projected on the chip.

CCD technology has been developed intensively since 1971 and has benefited from the general advances in the fabrication of silicon devices. CCDs are already being marketed by Intel, Fairchild and Texas Instruments. Development work is proceeding at Rockwell, Honeywell, Toshiba, Nippon Electric and other semiconductor manufacturers. Up to quarter-million word CCD-based serial memory systems have been developed as replacements for a rotating drum store.

CCDs have not been used in large numbers because as yet they have suffered from reliability problems and have little cost advantage over MOS RAM. They will begin to capture a significant share of the serial memory market when their cost per bit has dropped to less than half that of dynamic MOS RAM, the least expensive random access memory form (which is otherwise pre-ferred). Once this threshold has been reached, CCDs will find increasing use in large memory systems as buffer memories between mass magnetic storage and main memory, as well as in stand-alone applications such as small terminals and in memory-intensive microprocessor-based systems such as word-processing typewriters.

4.2.3   Magnetic Bubble

Magnetic bubble memory systems offer several advantages over conventional technologies:

- The non-volatility (data are retained when power is turned off);

- The high-bit packing density. Up to 10 million bits per square inch has been achieved and 100 million bits per square inch is possible;

- The low power consumption since one rotating in-place drive field can move many millions of bubbles;

- The ruggedness and small size of the all-solid state system;

- The excellent error rate (better than one to ten billion has been demonstrated).

Bubble technology has one intrinsic disadvantage: it is slower than semiconductor technology by about two orders of magnitude, especially if the bubble memory is organised to minimise cost (in long shift registers).

It appears that most manufacturers believe that they must achieve a chip capacity of at least 256,000 bits and a cost level of 0.01 cent/bit before their products will be viable. This, at today's state-of-the-art, implies two micron or smaller diameter bubbles and packaging in some conventional electronic formats. (The cost target is for the basic package and can be equated to the cost of semiconductor memory when purchased as 4K RAMs not yet assembled on a printed circuit board.)

This cost target will probably soon be achieved and surpassed, and chip capacities will evolve to and beyond the million-bit level in the early 1980s. Bubble memory systems will probably be offered to users by 1980 at costs of about 70 millicents per bit. Costs will then decline proportionally to those of semiconductors through the 1980s and then level off because of minimum bubble diameter limits: costs per bit should be one to eight millicents in the early 1990s varying widely with chip designs and access time.

Access times for bubble memories will not decrease as much, both because of inherent limitations and because other technologies will be preferred for higher speeds. We doubt that bubble memory random access times will ever be below five to eight microseconds in the lowest-cost systems.

4.2.4   Floppy Disks

Many word processors use the standard single density, single side diskette for text storage. These small inexpensive "floppy disks" are uniquely appropriate for handling text; they hold about 64 pages and can be easily filed in a folder with a final copy of the text itself. Although many word processors use the same physical diskette transport (Shugart, Memorex), there is very little similarity in the coding structure and formatting used. As a result, a diskette written by one word processor cannot be read by another. The most interesting development in this area has come with the announcement of IBM's Office System 6. That diskette is formatted such that the initial, or zero track appears to contain a format specification describing the structure of the disk itself. Thus, though the diskette formats are different from one IBM product to another, we can see IBM moving toward a general policy of "soft-loaded" disk handling capability: any disk drive would read the first track, call the appropriate software to handle that format and then proceed to read the disk. Another development in the area of diskettes will be the increased capacity of the diskette itself. Dual density diskettes are expected to be incorporated into new models over the next two years, doubling the capacity of the medium. Moreover, several manufacturers are expected to move in the direction of diskettes which record on both sides, thus doubling the capacity again. Whatever early limitations there may have been on the diskette – brittleness, increased error rate after long periods of storage – these appear to have been satisfactorily removed and we have little doubt that the diskette will, in one form or another, become the standard medium for local storage of text.

Typical costs of drives for floppy disks range from $230 for the mini size to $375 for the standard. Based largely on these prices, the cost per bit is 0.01 cent for the mini and 0.006 cent for the standard. A dual-density recording format is assumed, since it increases storage capacity without a significant increase in drive cost and probably will become quite common in a short time. Neither double-sided recording nor a double-track format is assumed, because the former requires a more expensive drive and the latter is highly sensitive to humidity, thermal expansion, and head positioning errors. The above costs include the drive electronics but not the controller; since controller chips that operate in conjunction with microprocessors are now becoming available, the controller is more appropriately considered part of the terminal.

4.2.5   Magnetic Disks

This discussion will focus on the larger units employing hard disks, since they lead the state-of-the-art. Smaller drives employing hard disks, and flexible ("floppy") disk drives, will improve roughly proportionally.

Huge strides have been made in cost reduction during the past ten years, principally through improvements in storage density. However, the practical limits have not yet been reached. Continued evolutionary improvements can be expected through the 1980s. Cost/bit will continue to be pressed in order to maintain a significant advantage over competing technologies. As a result, we expect major emphasis to be given to moving head drives, with the buffered approach used to compensate for the access time disadvantage of the moving head.

4.2.5.1   Moving Head Drives

The state-of-the-art of moving head drives is probably best described by the IBM 3350 which has a data storage density of roughly 3×10^6 bit/square inch. This is achieved through a linear recording density of roughly 6,000 bits/inch and a track density of 500 tracks/inch. The cost/bit for a 724 megabyte configuration is roughly 0.001 cent.

138

Something approaching an additional order of magnitude improvement in cost/bit can be expected in future moving head drives. Part of this will be achieved through increased storage densities. Linear recording densities in the order of 15,000 bits/inch appear to be practical in view of experimental results already reported. This increase will be obtained through a combination of improved media, reduced head-to-media spacing, and improved heads. Of the three parameters, the media and head-to-media spacing are most critical. Head performance is not the limiting factor. More uniform dispersions of smaller particle coatings with smoother finishes will be required. In addition, improved control of disk flatness and the dynamics of flying heads will be required. With evolutionary improvements in track zeroing systems, it is also likely that track densities will be increased to near 1,000 tracks/inch. The result of these improvements will be an increase in storage density to roughly 15×10^6 bits/square inch, or five times that presently available.

In addition to improvements in storage density, we also expect to see considerable effort devoted to system cost reduction. Some savings will be achieved through increased use of LSI with resulting savings in power supply, packaging, and interconnect components. Additional savings will be achieved through evolutionary improvements in mechanisms, materials and processing. A total system cost reduction in the order of 30 per cent is probably achievable.

As a result of these improvements by about 1990, large high density moving head drives should have a cost/bit approaching 0.0001 cent. In addition, capacities of 2,500 megabytes/drive should be available within the same sized enclosures. Access times will also be reduced perhaps 50 per cent through evolutionary improvements, but no significant improvement is anticipated in the drives themselves.

4.2.5.2 Fixed Head Drives

The potential introduction of competitive memory technologies with costs/bit similar to those of fixed head drives and with appreciably lower access times is expected to reduce the incentive for continued major development activity in this area. We do not expect to see cost improvements equivalent to those for moving head drives, so the fixed head disk will probably disappear.

4.2.6 Digital Tape Recording

Recording of digital data on small tape cassettes and cartridges is an established practice in the data processing and word processing fields. The major advantages of this approach are its relatively low cost per bit in large systems and the fact that the tape can be removed for long-term storage or the assembly of large files.

4.2.6.1. Magnetic Cassette Memories

Early digital cassette systems were simple modifications of audio recording systems, and they suffered because of it. Today's designs have higher reliability, operating speeds and bit packing densities, making them a viable option for a terminal. However, none of them is fast enough for direct support of any but the low-speed transmission channels.

Two kinds of cassettes are now in common use, the standard Philips cassette and the mini (dictation) cassette. The principal differences between them are that the former is manufactured to tighter dimensional tolerances and uses computer-grade (certified) tape. Both use 0.150-inch tape, provide two tracks and operate at a nominal bit packing density of 800 bpi. The standard cassette holds 300 feet of tape, the minicassette, 100 feet. Relatively inexpensive reel-to-reel drives are now available that provide good tape speed, while the minicassette is usually operated at uniform hub speed (variable tape speed).

4.2.6.2 Magnetic Cartridge Memories

Several kinds of magnetic cartridges have been introduced in recent years as alternatives to cassettes for off-line digital data storage. These have been designed specifically for data storage applications where high operating speeds and storage capacity are needed; they permit data transfer rates that are appreciably higher than those of cassettes and could directly support some medium-speed transmission channels.

1. One of the semiconductor or bubble memories would be best for buffer storage systems and systems for capturing coded text for soft display and small-format printout.

2. The digital tape and disk systems become attractive from a cost standpoint for larger blocks of information — typically fax in the smaller formats. The capacity of the individual media modules could prove awkward, however: thus, a key problem may be the development of automatic tape and disk changers, or the revision of the media standards to accommodate more data per module.

3. Practical utilisation of digital tape and disk systems for large quantities of fax and pictorial material will probably require the use of data compression hardware.

5.   INTELLIGENT COPIERS

5.1   Types of Equipment

The intelligent copier will be able to serve as:

- A local printer for a group of text processing terminals;
- A local printer for a remote data processing, word processing or communications system;
- A facsimile transceiver incorporating advanced optical character recognition and bandwidth compression;
- A convenience copier with capabilities such as contrast enhancement, zoom, edit and re-arrange.

Figure 5.1.A shows a block diagram of the smart copier. Actually, a single device, it simply disables some of its functions when it is working in the simpler modes. It can work directly as a subsystem of an integrated office communications system or, with the addition of a modem and perhaps a mass memory, can serve to buffer extended transmissions.

Partial prototypes of the smart copier already exist; recent products of Burroughs, Xerox and Matsushita incorporate several of the above features. We have just seen the first intelligent copiers arriving on the market:

1)   The IBM 6670 which does not yet have the facsimile capability.
2)   The Wang Intelligent Image Printer.

The capabilities of these smart copiers will be greatly expanded, however. They must have full graphic capability from the beginning (which implies the use of a xerographic, ink-jet, or other non-impact printer). But this capability will be steadily extended through large increases in working storage, graphic generator and software capability. A combination of optical character recognition and bandwidth compression will be essential to their economic use. Algorithms are likely to improve steadily and to be tailorable to the nature of a particular customer's traffic.

FIGURE 5.1.A

INTELLIGENT COPIER

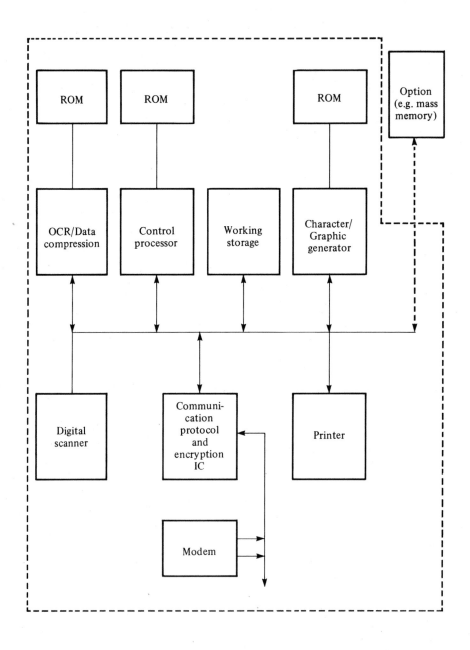

5.2   Technology

The best way to understand this is to look at the IBM 6670. This has:

- A copier-scanner using a laser and a photosensitive drum;

- Working storage, a fixed floppy disk, which can store up to 100 alphanumerical pages;

- A magnetic card reader compatible with IBM magnetic cards;

- SDLC couplers;

- A text image processor.

The IBM 6670 can be used as:

a)   An ordinary copier at 36 pages/minute.

b)   A printer accepting inputs from IBM magnetic cards and printing pages at 30 to 36 pages/minute using different type fonts and formats.

c)   A remote printer accessed by word processing machines or computer via SDLC lines to print text.

d)   Combining two input texts, from a computer data base and from another source, into one single document.

e)   Processor to improve image quality of data and print in reduced size.

f)   Double sided printer.

Printed document quality is rated as excellent.

5.3   Typical Prices

The IBM 6670 is priced at $75,000.

Wang's printer/copier, the Intelligent Image Printer, is priced at $35,000 but aiming at a lower range of the market than the IBM 6670.

Simple printer/copiers with facsimile capabilities could be in the $20,000 range by 1982.

There could also be some light duty versions costing less than $12,000 by 1982.

5.4 Main Manufacturers Selling in Europe Today

At present there is just IBM, and they are selling only in limited geographical markets.

5.5   Performance and Range of Application

The IBM 6670 can be considered as a high volume printer copier since its copier mechanism is the one used by the IBM Copier III which requires service only every 30,000 copies.

The initial Wang machine corresponded to a medium volume copier since some maintenance was required every 2,000 copies.

Other equipment whose price could be around $20,000 by 1982 would correspond to a medium volume copier. Equipment costing less than $12,000 would correspond to low volume copiers.

5.6 Expected and Possible Developments in the Next Decade

Influencing factors are:

1) Micro-electronics progress.
2) Wide-spread use of office copiers and text editing systems.
3) Development of the office of the future.

The high probability scenario runs as follows:

- Development of the use of text processing and editing machines and the need for office copiers will create the market for printer/copier systems. The printer/copier system will be developed into a general input/output document system where, in particular, facsimile and OCR functions will be added to large systems like the IBM 6670;

- The majority of printer/copier systems will have a transmit/receive function as an option.

Low probability scenario is:

- Printer/copiers do not evolve and do not find a market.

6. PRINTING TERMINALS

6.1 Types of Equipment

Three types of terminals are available to ARTEMIS users:

- Teleprinter;
- RJE terminal;
- High speed printers.

Most installed printer terminals are teletype compatible.

High speed printers, based on laser technology, are now appearing on the market for high volume printing jobs.

6.2   Technology

Teleprinters usually consist of a) a keyboard; b) a printing head and printing systems; c) a telecommunication interface; optionally, they may have a buffer, a paper tape reader/punch and storage. The protocol used by the terminal may be as simple as the basic teletype protocol or the IBM 2741 protocol with some form of error control. Transmission speeds are usually between 110 and 1,200 bps. There are also receive-only terminals (i.e. without keyboards).

RJE terminals usually consist of a) a printing head and a printing system; b) a telecommunication interface; c) a buffer; optional extras include a card reader and/or a keyboard and/or a mass memory. The protocol used by the terminal is usually of a bi-synch type or SDLC. Some RJE terminals are user-programmable so that the telecommunications protocol can be programmed.

Transmission speeds are usually between 2,400 bps and 9,600 bps.

"Traditional" *high speed line printers* operate at, typically, hundreds of lines per minute with a maximum of 1,400 lines per minute.

Very high speed printers use either laser printing or xerographic techniques. These very fast printers are controlled by a microcomputer and can print 20,000 lines per minute. (They are of course "receive-only" terminals.)

6.3   Printing System Techniques

6.3.1   Impact Printing

Impact printing is one of the most highly developed and widely accepted methods for converting an electronic digital code into alphanumeric text. Printing mechanisms are available to reproduce any quality of text desired from the least sophisticated 5 x 7 matrix characters for simple data listing to the best, fully-formed character printing of today's office typewriter. A key feature of this type of printing is that inexpensive paper can be used.

The conventional type-bar machine is not well suited to electronic drive. The most favourable alternatives for fully-formed character printing are the Selectric[R] type of mechanism for speeds in the range of ten to 30 characters per second and the daisy wheel configuration for speeds ranging up to 50 or 60 characters per second.

Daisy wheel printers are being produced in reasonably high volumes today. Industry sources as well as independent estimates place a minimum manufacturing cost of today's office-oriented designs at around $280 per unit, including the power supply. The cost is about equally divided between electronic and mechanical components.

A simple Selectric[R] type of electronically driven printer (again no keyboard or case) would have a manufacturing cost between $120 and $80, depending on whether it was the office or the consumer version. Almost all the expense would be in mechanical components.

Serial impact matrix printers often share the basic frame, carriage, and head transport mechanism with the daisy wheel system. The matrix architecture costs about ten per cent more than the daisy wheel systems in the 40 to 50 character per second range; when designed to operate at 300 to 400 characters per second, its cost is about 250 per cent more.

6.3.2   Thermal Printing

In recent years, there has been an extensive development of serial and line printing systems using a thermal matrix print head. These systems generally utilise papers coated with heat-reactive dyes that darken at temperatures between 100°C and 150°C. A matrix of small elements is in good thermal contact with paper, and the elements are selectively heated to form individual matrix characters. The heated elements are allowed to cool, and the print head is moved to the next column or character location.

Most systems utilise hybrid circuitry on silicon chips for the resistively heated elements. Writing speed is limited by the thermal time constant associated with each matrix element and the constraints on input power necessary to avoid overheating the print head package. Resolution is limited to about 75 elements per inch under the present state-of-the-art. Typical serial printing speeds are around 30 characters per second. If implemented in a line printing configuration, the speed could be raised to about 2,400 characters per second.

A different approach to thermal print head design has been implemented by using light-emitting diodes (LEDs) in conjunction with the conventional thermal printing paper. The low thermal mass of the heating elements allows higher modulation rates, but the low efficiency of the LEDs poses an even more severe heat dissipation problem in the print head.

The least expensive hardware for thermal printing would probably resemble today's low-cost teleprinters. The printing mechanism would serially print at rates up to 30 characters per second; the input would be a stream of character codes and the output a series of 5 x 7 matrix characters printed on a roll-fed web of coated paper 20 centimetres wide. Very limited graphics could be reproduced. Although some gray-scale reproduction might be possible, the contrast available is limited.

Using the current hardware as a model, today's design practice applied to high-volume production would produce the print mechanism and the associated electronics for about $120. About 80–85 per cent of that would be allocated to the electronic subsystem which decodes the input, generates the matrix characters and drives the paper feed and the print head motors. An all-out effort to produce a minimum-cost printer by restricting performance slightly and using innovative materials and fabrication methods could lead to a manufacturing cost of about $55, electronics still accounting for 70–75 per cent of the total.

The single print head itself represents only a small fraction of the total cost.

6.3.3   Electrosensitive Printing

Electrosensitive printing systems can provide a wide range of speeds and image quality. Some are designed for high-speed printing of utility-grade text, and others are intended for slower reproduction of high-quality facsimile images. In this technique, an electric current is passed through a writing stylus to remove or chemically modify the top coating on a specially prepared paper. The main advantage of this approach is the very low cost of the writing hardware, but it also produces high-contrast images and can reproduce a good-quality gray scale. This last feature has been extensively utilised in a number of facsimile systems, especially for news wirephotos and weather maps.

Most of the high-quality image work has been done with the traditional burn-off electrosensitive recording paper. This consists of a thick, opaque white layer (often a wax) applied over a black conducting layer. The electric current simply melts off the overcoat and exposes the undercoat where a black mark is desired. This recording is expensive and generates an objectionable amount of smoke and fumes if any quantity of recording is done. To overcome both cost and environmental problems, manufacturers are now marketing a paper that uses a very thin coating of aluminium instead of wax; however, this new product has a shiny metallic surface and produces images of low contrast.

If the environmental and cosmetic problems associated with the electrosensitive paper are overcome at reasonable cost, the technique offers an attractive hard-copy option. Used with a matrix printer for simple data, print speeds upward of 1,000 to 2,000 characters per second are possible. This could be achieved with hardware of approximately the same cost as the lower-throughput thermal systems discussed above.

Higher image quality (approximately 200 elements per inch) has been achieved at about 100 characters per second. Hardware costs should not be affected greatly if speed is reduced as the resolution is increased.

Although a system to produce pictorial material with gray-scale reproduction at rates of one to two square inches per second should be practical, none has yet appeared.

6.3.4   Ink-jet Printing

There have been a number of approaches to the formation and control of small jets of ink for non-contact printing on plain paper. Several ink-jet printing systems are commercially available for moderate-speed, high-quality text reproduction, colour plotting, and ultra-high-speed printing of utility-grade text. All of the devices are conceptually simple, but major challenges have arisen in connection with the practical problems of small-scale fabrication and ink composition.

The best available serial ink-jet printer produces high-quality text (240 elements per inch) at a rate of 92 characters per second. Higher speeds appear to be available at some sacrifice of resolution. The high cost of this equipment (above $20,000) is believed to be the result of an elaborate electronic system and a complex paper-handling system.

Another approach, presently being explored for computer printout applications, calls for a closely spaced array of fixed jets arranged to fully cover a moving paper web. This particular configuration is inherently less reliable than single-jet systems, but it could achieve a speed of more than ten pages per second.

The ink-jet is still too temperamental to be considered as the basis for a consumer product. However, if the current work leads to a successful and reliable system, this technology will have a decisive advantage. Not only will the technique offer flexibility in the type of text and graphics offered, but it will also be able to utilise inexpensive paper, even newsprint, and thereby minimise the cost of supplies. In addition, the hardware costs are seen to be potentially very low. The basic non-impact serial printer mechanism (frame, paper feed, print head carriage, electronics for character generation and control, etc) will be almost identical to the simple, inexpensive system described for thermal printing. If the technology is at all successful in developing a cost effective ink-jet print head, that component should add no more than $10 to the manufacturing cost associated with the coated-paper printers discussed previously.

6.3.5   Photosensitive Printers

There is a large family of photosensitive printing systems which respond to radiant energy but do not depend on temperature-induced effects.

The major categories of photosensitive systems include silver based emulsions, electrophotographic, dye-based, and photopolymer systems. The first method is too expensive and slow to develop automatically. Although the latter two systems are under intensive investigation for printing and micrographic systems, they appear to be at serious disadvantage in this application when compared with electrophotography. First, they are less sensitive by factors ranging from 10^3 to 10^6. This leads to either more expensive and complex exposure systems or a severely limited throughput. Second, the supplies costs are quite a bit higher, especially when compared with indirect electrophotography. Third, and possibly most significant, the long history and extensive experience with photocopiers makes electrophotography a far less risk-prone approach. This does not mean that other photosensitive systems will not be competitive, but it does suggest that electrophotography is the current standard.

Electrophotographic systems can be implemented in either of two modes:

- The indirect mode, in which the photosensitive material is part of the printer mechanism and the image is transferred to plain paper (e.g. plain-paper photocopiers); or

- The direct mode, in which the photosensitive material is part of the coated-paper recording medium (like the Electrofax or ZnO copier systems).

In either mode, throughput is not limited by the toning and fixing processes — more than 100 pages per minute are possible with today's techniques. Indirect, dry toner systems, the poorest in terms of resolution, typically provide images equivalent to 250–350 elements per inch.

Several writing mechanisms are available. A modulated laser beam scanned over the image area by an oscillating or rotating mirror system has already been used by several facsimile and computer printer designers. As the cost of the laser diodes and the associated drive circuitry come down, an array of modulated light sources stretched across the page becomes a possibility. Current projections do not show a significant difference in cost between these two scanning systems.

Few of these systems excel in reproducing pictorial material containing shades of gray. Although some photoconductors have shown outstanding continuous-tone capability, most of the commercial processes operate in a high-contrast mode. Nevertheless, reproduction of coarse halftone pictures is possible with the plain paper equipment, and the coated paper approaches offer quite adequate halftone performance for this application due to their superior resolving power.

6.3.6   Electrostatic Printing

For computer-oriented printing and plotting, a number of systems have been developed in which electrostatic forces are used to deposit ink or toner to form an image. The most common of these deposit an electric charge directly on a dielectric-coated paper using a linear array of electrodes. As the paper moves under the array, the individual electrodes are energised to form a charged image. Toner is then deposited on the image and fixed to produce a permanent image on the paper.

Reliable, good quality, multi-stylus writing of this type is routinely achieved at 200 elements per inch. Currently, resolution is limited by electrode fabrication techniques. More advanced technology might improve the resolution by a factor of two or more, but it would require a substantial investment. Inter-digitation and overlap of dot patterns are probably better paths to follow for improved image quality.

Most commercial systems operate at fairly low speeds (in the order of ten to 15 pages per minute), but the basic technique is capable of ten times that.

Indirect electrostatic printing has been proposed in which the charge image is created and toned on an intermediate dielectric surface; the toned image is then transferred to plain paper, where it is fixed. Results with laboratory equipment are quite encouraging. If it can be perfected, this approach would result in a plain paper electrostatic printer which might prove slightly less expensive than its electrophotographic counterpart, because the writing system might be less expensive.

Experiments have shown the feasibility of generating 15 to 20 shades of gray with an electro-static printing system. Although it uses a more complex electrode structure, this advanced system still offers speed and resolution capabilities on a par with the conventional configurations.

6.4   Typical Prices

Teleprinters:

Basic teleprinter	around $1,200
Buffered teleprinter	around $3,000
Teleprinter with bubble memory	around $3,500

RJE Terminals:

Typical prices	$20–30,000

High Speed Printers:

Prices vary very much:

IBM 3800	$320,000
Honeywell PPS	$200,000

6.5　Performance and Range of Applications

6.5.1　Teleprinters

The basic teleprinter has a printing speed in the order of 30 characters/second, while faster teleprinters can have a printing speed of up to 120 characters/second.

Basic teleprinters are not very well suited to receive texts since the printing speed is not fast enough. It seems advisable that incoming documents be received on local buffer memory before being printed.

6.5.2　RJE Terminals

These terminals are primarily intended to receive large amounts of information which has been processed by computer. Printing speeds of these terminals are of the order of a few hundred characters per second, so they are well suited to receive large amounts of information.

6.5.3　High Speed Printers

These usually print information directly from computers. Their performance restricts them to organisations where printing is concentrated. They can in fact be used as an in-plant printing centre. Typical performance: $1-18,000$ lines/minute.

6.6 Expected and Possible Developments in the Next Decade

We do not expect the price to go down. Prices should remain about the same since the majority of the cost is due to the electromechanical part of the terminal.

However, we expect that:

1) Simple teleprinters will be provided with memory systems (the Texas Instruments silent terminal is a typical example).

2) Batch terminals are not going to be as successful as in the past since the development of the cheap decentralised intelligent terminal is going to hurt their traditional market.

3) High speed printers will have their price reduced.

7. TEXT AND IMAGE COMPRESSION

7.1 Scope

This Appendix deals with operations performed on text — i.e. strings of characters — or on images, such as maps, letters, documents, drawings or pictures, that allow the text or images to be stored or transmitted in fewer bits than the original, without loss of information content. *Text* is usually compressed without distortion, so the original can be reconstructed exactly from the compressed form; *image* compression, however, takes advantage of the properties of the human visual system to achieve a satisfactory compressed image even though the original cannot be precisely reconstructed from it.

7.2 Current State-of-the-art

7.2.1 Text

Apart from elementary procedures such as abbreviation — e.g. "NY" for "New York" — in a text in which no other element is abbreviated in the same way, there are two general classes of compression in use: pattern substitution and statistical encoding.

In *pattern substitution,* the compressed text is formed by replacing certain recurring patterns in the original text, such as runs of zeros or blanks, by shorter, fixed patterns. Alternatively, the recurring patterns may be digraphs (pairs of characters) and the replacements may be single characters; for example, the digraph AS in English text may be replaced by an ASCII (eight-bit) character that is otherwise unused. By extension, recurring strings of lengths 2, 3, 4, ... characters in the original text may be replaced by shorter, but fixed, strings in the compressed text.

With digraph substitution by single characters, the highest possible compression ratio, or ratio of size of original file to size of compressed file is 2; typically, a ratio of 1.5 to 1.8 is achieved. This kind of compression is quite simple to program, and takes little storage and execution time. At the cost of greater overhead, pattern substitution for strings of a greater range of lengths can achieve ratios of 2.4 for English text, and higher for other types of original text.

Statistical encoding is the substitution in the compressed text of short symbols for frequently-recurring elements of the original text and longer symbols for those that occur infrequently. Morse code is a familiar example, since the frequently-occurring E is "." and the less-frequently occurring H is "....". The prototypical, widely used code is the Huffman code, which has the following theoretical property of interest: it is the *optimal prefix code,* that is, it achieves the greatest possible compression, for a given source alphabet, among all codes with the "prefix property": codes in which no code element is the prefix of another and thus in which decoding is relatively simple. When the source alphabet is English text, consisting of 26 letters, blank and punctuation, the compression possible with practical Huffman codes is close to the theoretical limit.

This limit is determined by the entropy of the text, or

$$H = -\sum_{1}^{M} p_i \ log_2 \ p_i$$

where p_i = probability of occurrence of i-th character in the source text, and M = the number of different characters in the source alphabet e.g. 27 for 26 letters and blank. For English, $H \simeq$ 2.4 bits per character. Thus, relative to common codes such as ASCII and EBCDIC that have 8 bits per character, a Huffman code can achieve a compression ratio of 8/2.4 = 3.3.

The potential compression ratio for a Huffman or other statistical code is not so great if the source text approaches an equiprobable distribution of characters. For example, if in English the 27 characters all occurred with probability $1/27$, the greatest compression ratio achievable with a Huffman code, relative to ASCII or EBCDIC, would be 1.7. Conversely, the Huffman code performs very well if the source alphabet probabilities are highly skewed. To generate a Huffman code, the user must obtain the source character frequency statistics; if these change over time, the code should be adjusted to maintain optimal compression, but the sensitivity of code structure to normal changes in statistics is generally not high for a given data base.

The run-time compression and decompression operations for a Huffman code are somewhat more complex than for pattern substitution, and more computation is needed initially to discover the proper source alphabet and to generate the code.

A source text that has already been partially compressed by pattern substitution, such as run-length encoding, can subsequently be subjected to Huffman encoding to achieve still greater overall compression.

7.2.2   Images

Schemes for image compression are generally rated according to a subjective criterion: the degree to which the compressed image is useful to a human being, since images are viewed by human beings. These subjective criteria have not been systematically developed. For two-tone images, exemplified by typewritten or handwritten letters, schematic drawings, weather maps and the like, the CCITT has made up a number of test images that are used in evaluating facsimile transmission systems. A particular compressed image can be judged by comparison with the original, in terms of legibility or resolution of detail. For pictures, exemplified by photographs and individual frames of a video signal*, the subjective criteria are more complex and application-dependent, and have not been well established. For example, the resolution in a photograph desired by the reader of a newspaper is different from that required by an analyst of an intelligence photograph from a satellite. Quite often, owing to the lack of knowledge about the objective equivalents of impairments, criteria such as mean-square error are applied, although they have not been "calibrated" against subjective judgements.

When images are converted to digital form, they are more readily handled by digital computers, for such operations as storage, retrieval and encryption; also, they are better suited for the digital transmission media, such as pulse code modulation (PCM) carriers, that have become dominant in the last 20 years. These are the techniques relevant to ARTEMIS, so this section deals only with compression techniques applicable to images in digital form.

*We do not deal with images of moving objects

For two-tone images, each picture element, or "pel", is assumed to have the value 1 or 0, corresponding to black or white. Since the subjectively desirable resolution for various classes of two-tone images is in the range of 40 points, or pels, per centimetre (p/cm) to 400 p/cm, and since the original images are typically A4 pages, the complete original image contains about one million to 100 million bits (Mb). It is thus necessary in practical compression schemes to look for methods that require the storage of only a small portion of the image. One practical scheme, run length encoding in one dimension, uses a Huffman code to symbolise the lengths of runs of black and white pels. Since only one dimension is scanned, the storage of only one scan line, or about 8,000 bits at 400 p/cm is required. The maximum attainable compression factor is determined by the source image entropy; it is about 12 for such images as weather maps and printed text, with a low resolution of about 40 p/cm and a typical page occupancy of 25 per cent (i.e. one quarter of the page occupied by significant portions of the image). At higher resolutions, the compression factor for one-dimensional scanning diminishes, and two-dimensional methods are needed to obtain appreciable compression factors. One such method is predictive differential quantising (PDQ), in which the difference in black and white run lengths between two successive scan lines is symbolised by a Huffman code; two lines, or about 16,000 bits at 40 p/cm, must be stored. This method requires greater complexity to program and execute than run length encoding. The achievable compression ratio is in the range of 12 to 18 at 400 p/cm again assuming 25 per cent page occupancy. As in the case of run length encoding, these values are close to the theoretical upper limits that can be estimated from the entropy of the source image. We emphasise that the entropies in the two cases, run length coding and PDQ, are quite different: in the first case, the probabilities are those of changes in run lengths over two successive scan lines. Obviously, in either case, the measurement or estimation of the required probabilities is a complex task, requiring scanning of the source image and computer analysis. For a given class of images, such as weather maps, this is carried out only once.

In more complex images, such as monochrome or colour photographs, each pel has a continuous range of intensity values, rather than just the 1 or 0 of two-tone images. To illustrate the uncompressed information content of such pictures, a monochrome image with 1,000 pels resolution in both horizontal and vertical dimensions, typical of a small, high-definition photograph, contains 8 Mb when each pel is quantised to one of 256 levels (8-bit quantisation); a colour image with lesser resolution, 250 pels in each dimension, contains 1.5 Mb when the intensity for each of three primary colours per pel is similarly encoded. With some sacrifice of quality, monochrome pictures may be encoded with fewer bits per pel, say six to eight; the corresponding range for colour pictures, which require three times as many bits per pel at the same resolution, is 18 to 25 bits per pel.

Several adaptive coding techniques exist. In these, the image is scanned in two dimensions; the resulting two-dimensional analogue signal is converted to a two-dimensional digital form (A/D conversion); and the two-dimensional digital representation is quantised and encoded in an efficient way into a one-dimensional bit stream. The efficiency results from allotting more bits to "active" parts of the picture, with large amounts of detail and many tone transitions, and fewer bits to quiet areas of the picture, such as uniform background. Owing to the limitations of storage in practical processors and also of computational speed (since many computations must be carried out per image), images are usually scanned in blocks of the order of 32 by 32 pels up to 256 by 256 pels, resulting in somewhat less overall compression than would be possible if the entire image could be processed at once. There have been demonstrations of adaptive coding systems which achieve good subjective picture quality at bit rates of 0.5 to 1.0 bit per pel for monochrome pictures, and one to two bits per pel for colour, implying compression ratios of eight to 16 for monochrome and 12 to 24 for colour. The overhead information needed to decode the images is only a few per cent of the total that is transmitted or stored, and the processing is rapid enough to permit tens to hundreds of images per second to be handled, as in video transmission.

7.3   Environmental Forcing Functions

There are two advantages of text or image compression: the reduction of the storage required for a given original item, and the reduction of the product of time and bandwidth needed to transmit it. These advantages appear in various aspects of information-handling systems. For example, text compression not only reduces the amount of mass storage required for large data bases, it also reduces the input/output time required of the computer in storing and retrieving the data. The implications for communications costs are also evident.

For text, the principal characteristic which makes it eligible for compression is its entropy. If text expressed in an eight-bit code such as ASCII has entropy of, say, five bits per character, there is less to be gained (lower compression ratio) in compression than if it has two bits of entropy per character. Since the entropy is widely different for English text, computer program code, numerical data, and so forth, the user must know the text characteristics beforehand. From the practical viewpoint, it is more worthwhile to implement compression schemes for a text data base such as ARTEMIS where the total quantity of data is large and its use will continue for some time.

With respect to pictures, the reduction in the product of time and bandwidth for transmission that results from compression is especially important. Typical applications today are in commercial facsimile, to reduce transmission time and hence cost, on the telephone network, space communication, in which the power-bandwidth product of space vehicles is at a premium and military systems, in which images must be sent over media with limited bandwidth, such as troposcatter radio. Although there are theoretical limits due to source entropy on the compression ratio for images, the state-of-the-art is limited more by processing and storage technologies.

7.4   Technological Environment

Text compression, even in its more advanced forms such as Huffman coding, uses relatively straightfoward software; for example, digraph substitution is not greatly different from computer routines for "packing" data, which is an elementary form of compression. There is no practical difficulty in achieving compression ratios close to the theoretical maximum indicated by the source entropy. As the cost per operating cycle of a computer and cycle time decrease, it will become more attractive to compress data. On the other hand, if the costs of mass memory and the costs per unit bandwidth of communications media also decrease, there will be less payoff in compressing data.

The incentive to compress images will probably prevail, since the quantity of images per user has tended to increase with such applications as large-scale and long-range weather forecasting and earth surveillance from satellites. Fast and inexpensive memory and logic — e.g. in microprocessors — will contribute to the development of more complex image compression techniques, although it seems likely that, for some time, the degree of compression will be limited by the exceptionally large number of computations per pel that are required.

7.5   Forecasts

7.5.1.   1980–1985

Text compression with both simple (pattern substitution) and advanced (statistical encoding) methods will continue to be applied to large and very large data bases, principally to reduce mass storage requirements. Special-purpose LSI chips will be produced for Huffman coding.

Analogue methods of storing and transmitting images will be replaced almost entirely by digital methods.

Commercial digital facsimile equipment using two-tone image compression, with combinations of one-dimensional and two-dimensional scanning techniques, will produce one A4 page per 30 to 60 seconds, with medium to high quality, at 4,800 bits per second (bps).

The subjective effects of image impairments, especially for complex images such as photographs, will be further studied and reduced to approximate objective equivalents, much as has been done in voice communication, leading to a better understanding of compression techniques and hence to higher compression ratios at a given cost.

Experimental image compression systems for monochrome and colour photographs will be demonstrated and applied to a limited extent, with compression ratios of about ten to 20.

7.5.2   1986–1995

Text compression will compete with alternative techniques for managing large data bases, and will be relegated to a secondary role, owing to the reduced costs of mass storage and faster data access techniques.

(Medium and low probability) Digital facsimile at less than 4,800 bps will operate over public switched networks – e.g. the telephone system or alternative digital networks, at the minute-per-page rate.

(Low probability) Advanced techniques for adaptive encoding of pictures, using extremely fast computer and storage, will result in compression ratios of 20 to 40.

BIBLIOGRAPHY

1. HOLBOROW, C et al. A Review of Data Compression Algorithms. 1st May 1976. NTIS Document AD/A–035 786

2. ARONSON, J. Data Compression – A Comparison of Methods. June 1977. NBS Special Publication 500–12

3. HABIBI. A. Survey of Adaptive Image Coding Techniques. *IEEE Transactions on Communications* COM–25 (11): 1275–1284, November 1977

4. CHEN, W.H. and SMITH, C.H. Adaptive Coding of Monochrome and Colour Images. Ibid 1285–1292

5. HUANG, T.S. Coding of Two-tone Images. Ibid 1406–1424

6. MUSMANN, H.G. and PREUSS, D. Comparison of Redundancy Reducing Codes for Facsimile Transmission of Documents. Ibid 1425–1433

8. DOCUMENT QUALITY

8.1 Introduction

The effectiveness of a document fulfilment service will be measured by the user against three criteria:

- Cost;
- Speed;
- Quality.

The first two of these are intuitively obvious and are not discussed in this Appendix. The third is a lot more complex and is analysed here.

To take a simplified view of the preparation of a journal article, four functions are undertaken respectively by the:

- Author;
- Editor;
- Compositor;
- Printer.

In the process of reproduction to fulfil the request for a document, some part of the contribution of each of these may be destroyed. For example, the quality of the paper, the presence of colour or even the typeface may be changed.

The user may be prepared to wait and/or pay more to preserve certain characteristics of the original in his copy. But he may actually prefer the modified version, choosing, for example, to have a microfilm copy because it is cheaper to mail and store.

This Appendix discusses these concepts of quality in order to provide an insight into the reasons for choice of technology in a document digitalisation system. Once a document has been digital-ised, the storage and transmission of *all* the information in the digitalised version is always possible. However, the reproduction process itself may not use all the information. For example, the output device may not be able to reproduce colour.

8.2   The Preparation of Original Documents

8.2.1   Simplified Overview

The author of a scientific or technical paper normally presents a typescript accompanied by diagrams and perhaps photographs, which may be in colour, to the editor of the journal in which it will be published. Following reviews, corrections and editing, a final typescript is prepared and the author's work is finished (unless he checks the galley proofs).

The editor determines the rules for typesetting and the reproduction of graphic material, and indicates on the typescript how they are to be applied. This process adjusts the author's typescript to the house style.

The compositor sets the type and lays out the pages according to the editor's instructions. He adjusts line lengths, hyphenates words, numbers pages, pastes in graphics and so on to provide the "form" of the document.

The printer reproduces the composed pages as many times as required on the appropriate size and quality of paper, collates, staples or binds and delivers the completed version.

We have ignored numerous other contributors, such as artists and blockmakers, advertisers and advertisement editors, who might have a part to play. Each may add some information to the final package through his participation. It is to this "information" that attention is now turned.

Information is the subject of a complete body of scientific theory. Some of the laws of information theory have a direct relevance here.

The first crucial conclusion of information theory is that no information handling system can restore information that has been lost through prior processing. If, for example, a colour diagram is copied in black and white, no machine can restore the original colour using only the black and white copy as input. A telephone cannot transmit a nod and a wink! In effect, the best copy cannot be better than the original.

The second conclusion states that an information system must be able to recognise a difference by behaving differently if the "variety" represented by the difference is to be preserved. If, for example, a typewriter uses the same character for letter O and number zero, no machine can tell the difference (and neither can a human without reference to the context). In particular, an OCR reader (which relies on Optical Character Recognition) would not know which code to store in a computer.

A document fulfilment system which reproduces originals from its centre as copies at a distance by digitalising, storing and transmitting information, is at best able to reproduce the variety of information available at its most degraded point in the process.

8.2.2   Information from the Author

The author's typescript contains information in the form of words, symbols, punctuation, diacritical marks, diagrams, pictures and possibly layout (e.g. line lengths for poetry, lists or bold type).

In general, an author's message (here meaning a set of information) can be conveyed by an original document, tearsheet, reprint, copy, Viewdata screen or microfilm. It probably does not matter to the user whether he reads the first edition hardback or reset paperback, a presentation copy or a photocopy. However, any device that the author exploited to convey information must be preserved, or the document edited to convey the same message in another way. For example, coloured lines on graphs may be redrawn as dotted, dashed or solid black lines. Mathematical notation is a particularly important feature of much scientific and technical publishing.

The author's information — carrying devices are:

Words	Spelling
	Phonetic renderings
	Capitalisation
	Character sets (mathematics, Greek letters ...)
Syntax and Sentences Structure	Paragraphs
	Lists
	Headings
	Chapters
Graphics	Diagrams, line drawings
	Halftones
	Photographs
	Colour

8.2.3   Information from the Editor and Compositor

The division of duties between these two will vary. However, between them, they choose and establish:

Typeface
Page numbers
Margins
Page size and paper size
Line length and words/page
Running titles

Contd......

Hyphenation
Page layout — Pictures
                    Adjacent articles
                    Advertisements
Cross references to "this, previous or forthcoming" issues.

The presence of an article in a particular journal may also add meaning or give status to it. So too may the position of the item on the page or within the bound volume. This context is conveyed by the editor as representative of the publisher.

Other features of occasional relevance in this area are misprints, colour coding of paper, legibility, cachet and honour to author, juxtaposition of related articles. The majority of users of STI would not normally need to see the rest of the journal to place an individual article in context.

8.2.4   Information from the Printer and Publisher

The final processes of printing and publishing add the following;

        Paper quality (or microfilm)
        Binding (hard, stapled, soft, looseleaf ....)
        Ink texture (e.g. Intaglio) and colour
        Stereoscopic diagrams
        Scent impregnated paper
        Book numbers and catalogue reference
        Jackets

Coffee table books and folio editions, incunabula, signed and first editions, rare manuscripts and the like have value in their form as well as content. The previous owners and readers may be significant too. (Fermat's celebrated Last Theorem was a margin note in another mathematician's work- well thumbed edges guide the eye to the most salacious pages in works of erotica).

We can presume that a document fulfilment centre will not be concerned with this class of information. Schrlars will continue to visit libraries and special collections in person.

8.3 Copies, Facsimiles and Forgeries

8.3.1 Improving on the Original

The user may not want the original, even if it were available at an acceptable price and soon enough. He may prefer microfilm to paper for its small size or vice versa for reading without machinery.

Other possibilities include:

- More readable script — modern, not Gothic; Braille; large type; romanised Cyrillic;

- Image enhancement from photographs;

- Format compatible with other material;

- Excerpts and extracts;

- Re-sequencing and juxtapositioning;

- Mechanical translation.

An electronic fulfilment service may well be used as much for these kinds of "enhanced" service as for its more faithful-to-the-original copy service.

8.3.2 Perfect Copies

The model against which a reproduction must be measured for this service is an item printed by the publisher in his normal print run.

If ARTEMIS proves successful, it may well be the only way in which some documents are ever published. The original in this case would be electronic, not printed.

A perfect "distributed intelligent copier" could take banknotes as input and produce undetectable forgeries as output. However, neither ink nor paper would be available to the user of the proposed fulfilment service. The upper limit of perfection will probably be similar to that achieved on today's plain paper copiers — either colour or black and white. Copying bureaux and in-house printing/reprographics centres will be able to maintain this quality if their machines are kept in good order and have suitable interfaces.

8.3.3   Facsimiles and Photocopies

The quality of facsimiles and photocopies is determined by two factors: resolution and intensity discrimination. Both of these are discussed in Appendix 7 — Text and Image Compression.

For a black and white image only, each picture element ("pel") requires only one data bit to represent its colour. However, to describe different shades of gray, six to eight bits, which distinguish 64 or 256 shades (2^6 or 2^8) may be needed.

For a coloured image, the intensity of each of three primary colours must be recorded, which requires three times as many bits.

The number of "pels" on a page determines the resolution. The human eye cannot use more information than is provided by 400 points per centimetre without magnifying the image. Quite acceptable images can be achieved with 40 points per centimetre, if a cheap but legible document is all that is required.

Fulfilment centres often meet requests by making photocopies. Colour and gray tones are not preserved, but the document is readable.

Colour copies have now achieved such high fidelity that forgers have used them for financial certificates indicating a level of image quality acceptable to a very discriminating reader.

8.3.4   Equivalent Texts

For scientific and technical information dissemination, an accurate version of a text, which ignores format entirely, may be quite adequate, particularly where no diagrams are involved.

Text processing systems can print essentially the same information with different type faces, line and page lengths, hyphenation and so on. The input to the system could have been by optical recognition of characters in yet another format and typeface.

These "equivalent texts" contain all the author's and much of the editor's contribution to the information content of the article (always excepting graphics).

Much of the STI handled by ARTEMIS is likely to be of this kind because it is economical to store and transmit and cheap to collect as a by-product of text preparation.

8.3.5   Revisions, Extracts and Translations

It is usually important to a reader to know if he has an original version or a revision of a text. When borrowing from a library, he may even specify, say, the original hardback not the later paperback because the former contains pictures, or vice versa because the latter has some later material, making it a new edition.

The same material may appear as a reprinted journal article, an extract in an anthology, a revised and reset edition or a substantial quotation in another work. Users of ARTEMIS may need the ability to specify which of these they want, or may choose to leave the system to deliver any version, provided that it indicates clearly both the existence of other versions and which one it has provided.

Synopses and abstracts are essentially bibliographic and SDI (selection dissemination of information) tools, rather than "low quality" versions of the original material.

Translations try to capture the complete information content of the original, and are obviously more valuable to some readers than the original itself. However, some figures of speech, such as puns, may defy translation. One of ARTEMIS's main contributions could ultimately be its ability to deliver texts in original languages along with literal but usable machine translations.

9.   TELECOMMUNICATIONS TECHNOLOGY AVAILABLE TO ARTEMIS

9.1   Range of Relevant Technologies

To build up a suitable network for document transmission, one may consider basically:

1)   TDM circuit switching technology.

2)   Packet switching technology.

3)   TDM circuit switching technology with statistical multiplexing i.e. hybrid technology.

Comments:

- Circuit switching technology has been used not only in telephone systems but also for data networks such as NDN, EDS/IDN;

- Packet switching technology was proved feasible in the early 1970s (Arpa, Sita, RCP) and used for public data switched networks, such as Transpac, Telenet, Datapac and Euronet;

- Hybrid technology is not very widespread, but some commercial networks have been using it: Saponet, Mondesion.

The basis of all network technologies is digital transmission.

9.1.1.   Circuit-switching

The trend is naturally to go digital. However, the introduction of digital switches in the national telephone network has been relatively slow and it is only since 1976 that digital switching has been globally accepted as the leading telephone switching technology:

- A stored program control system is now a required standard by users and manufacturers;

- Stored program control makes use of either a highly centralised processor or distributed processing power within the system;

- The switching matrix can be implemented using electromechanical devices like reed relays, semiconductor devices like MOS cross-points, or using time division multiplexing (TDM) techniques allowing switching through time-dependent gates;

- However, with the rapid development of microelectronics in terms of improved performance and reduced costs, the TDM technique is accepted as the trend in the field of switching and telephony;

- TDM switching systems, which were first introduced for large transit and local switches, are now developed for the whole range of switching systems. Even for a PABX with more than 100 to 200 lines, TDM now proves to be globally more economical than the other analogue techniques such as PAM and PWM (Pulse Amplitude Modulation, and Pulse Width Modulation). For very large switching systems today, the switching matrix is often implemented through a combination of time and space switching.

- *Conclusion:*

  Modern circuit switching systems are controlled by stored programs and use TDM for switching the information they receive. Other technologies based on analogue switching are no longer favoured and will soon be no longer manufactured.

9.1.2   Packet-switching

There are today two main families of technologies: one is based on the autonomous packet and one on the virtual link concept. In the autonomous packet mode, each packet is sent individually within the network according to the routing information attached to it.

In the virtual link mode, a path is pre-established within the network and each packet of the related communication will use the pre-established path.

The main advantage of the autonomous packet mode is that it requires less memory and less CPU power than the virtual link mode.

Conversely, the main advantage of the virtual link mode is a better capability for flow control and congestion control, with less overhead.

However, with the progress of micro-electronics, it has become more economical today to invest in data handling and thereby save bandwidth which is relatively more costly. This trend is illustrated by the relative cost trends observed in the telecommunications field where terrestrial line costs are decreasing at a rate of about 15 per cent, and in the computer industry where the rate is much faster.

Furthermore, while the first packet switching nodes were based on off-the-shelf minicomputers, the packet swtching nodes are now based on especially-developed telecommunications architectures like the Transpac nodes for the French public data network or the Telenet nodes for the Telenet network. These new machines enable the network to achieve greater processing performance.

The above trends are partially responsible for the shifts from autonomous packet mode toward the virtual link mode.

- *Conclusion:*

  Today, the packet network technique most likely to be selected is the one based on the virtual link mode.

9.1.3 Hybrid switching

There are not many examples of hybrid switching techniques in commercial operations and one cannot claim at present that a given hybrid technique is much better than any other available one.

9.2 Description of Each Variant

9.2.1 Circuit Switching

An example of a network currently available for document transmission is the Nordic Data Network. This gives switched service to asynchronous and synchronous data terminals from 300 to 9,600 bps. The mode of operation is full duplex and the interface between the data terminal equipment (DTE) and the data communications equipment (DCE) uses a four-wire circuit. The protocols used to gain access to the network are basically X21 and V24.

The main service provided is transparent synchronous full duplex transmission. The network is independent of the telephone network and has been built mainly for medium speed CCITT Number 5 data terminals.

By 1985, this network will have 13 nodes, 270 circuit concentrators, 260 remote multiplexers and around 55,000 DCEs. The nodes are based on the Ericsson Axe 30 system which is a TDM electronic circuit switch using 60 + 4 kbps circuits. The network is fully synchronised and uses an 8 + 2 bit envelope for transmission. The transmission facilities are analogue circuits.

Performance:

Call set up time:	below 100 milliseconds for 90 per cent of the calls
Call clearing:	below 50 milliseconds for 90 per cent of the calls
Node:	at least 100 calls/second.

9.2.2 Packet Switching

An example of a network available for document/data transmission is the French national data network Transpac. This network provides switched service to asynchronous and synchronous data terminals from 100 bauds up to 48K bps. The mode of operation is full duplex and the interface between the DTE and the DCE normally uses a four-wire circuit. Normal access to the network is via a leased line but one can have access to the network via the telephone or telex networks as well.

The standard access protocol is X25; however, the Transpac network can also be accessed by asynchronous terminals since it supports the X28 and X29 standards for a PAD Protocol.

The main service provided is the virtual circuit service whereby information transmitted in the form of packets is received in the proper sequence by the receiving DTE.

The network transmission scheme is based on virtual end-to-end circuits established within the network. Each circuit is established at call set up and each packet of information follows the same link.

Flow control is achieved through individual step-by-step control of each communication. The internode protocol is a kind of multilink balanced X25. Internode trunks are at 72K bps over analogue lines.

Performance:

Call set up:	less than 1.5 seconds
Network transit time:	average around 200 milliseconds
Present node throughput:	0.5 to 1 megabits/second

9.2.3   Hybrid Switching

An example is provided by Tran equipment. The network is based on TDM and is fully synchronised. Asynchronous and synchronous terminals can be connected.

Two services are provided:

a)   Transparent virtual circuit service where the terminals communicating through this virtual circuit are operating as if interconnected by a leased line having a bit rate comparable to that used by the two terminals (TDM circuit switching).

b)   Statistically multiplexed minipackets on an end-to-end transparent virtual circuit service. Asynchronous terminals and synchronous terminals using a standard access protocol — e.g. X25 (which provides error protection), are supported.

Such a network has been established by the South African PTT to provide both circuit switching and packet transmission.

9.3.   Comparison of Packet and Circuit Switching

9.3.1   Criteria for Comparison

Technical:

A)   Network performance (see 9.3.2 below):

— Network transit delay;
— Network availability;
— Congestion control/flow control;
— Transparency and access protocols;
— Overhead;
— Bandwidth required.

B)   Network transport services (see 9.3.3 below):

— Call set up time;
— Type of services (virtual circuit, other);
— Throughput with respect to bandwidth;
— Error protection;
— Speed conversion;
— Protocol conversion;
— Priority handling.

Economics (see 9.3.4 below):

Cost apportionment within a network;
General technico-economic trends;
Maintenance.

9.3.2   Technical Comparison — Network Performance

Transit delay within the network is much lower for circuit-switched nodes than packet-switched nodes at present.

For a circuit-switched network: transit delay = propagation delay

For a packet-switched network: transit delay = propagation delay + propagation of one packet (typical 100—200 milliseconds at 50K bps).

However, the picture could change, should the packet network use T1 digital trunks at 1.5 or 2M bps).

Call set up time is higher on a packet network than on a circuit network.

Network Availability

A packet network using the autonomous packet mode should provide a more reliable service than a circuit network.

A packet network using the virtual link mode has greater availability than a circuit network since its connectivity can be higher at lower cost.

Congestion Control/Flow Control

In a circuit network, congestion control is mainly achieved by rejection of calls above a certain threshold.

In an autonomous packet network, it is difficult to prevent congestion. The mechanism normally used involves end-to-end flow control which is difficult to relate to network node congestion and call rejection.

In a virtual link packet network, congestion control is easily achieved and proper bandwidth rationing for the various communications within a congested network area can be achieved.

Transparency and Access Protocol

The protocol for access to a circuit-switched network is relatively simple (e.g. X21). It is basically a call set up/call clear protocol. As soon as the DTE-DTE communication is established, the network is transparent to any type of digitised information which can be exchanged by the two DTEs provided it meets the allocated bit rate.

The access protocol of a packet network, in contrast, is more elaborate (e.g. X25). The protocol must be implemented within the computer access method and terminals, or costly protocol conversions must be made. So an advantage of a circuit-switched network for closed system working is its transparency to protocols defined by users or manufacturers.

Overhead

For a circuit-switched network during the transmission phase between two DTEs, the information transmitted carries no overhead.

For a packet network, each packet carries overhead information (link control, error control, synchronous flag or character routing information, etc). This amounts sometimes to 15–20 per cent extra traffic.

Bandwidth Required

Except for overhead, packet switching makes efficient use of the transmission resources since these resources are dynamically allocated, whilst circuit switching pre-allocates a fixed bandwidth or bit rate whether the two DTEs are effectively exchanging information or not. This is particularly important for conversational terminals and time-sharing terminals. The line or circuit occupancy of a conversational CRT terminal is around four per cent and the line or circuit occupancy of time-sharing is less than ten per cent.

- Packet switching offers large bandwidth savings for these types of terminals;

- For asynchronous (TTY-like terminals), packet switching brings substantial bandwidth savings compared with circuit switching, but incurs a high overhead since the asynchronous data packets are very often not full length packets;

- Whilst circuit switching can use 100 per cent of its bandwidth, packet switching can only use 70 per cent to 80 per cent of it, to avoid excessive queueing delays.

9.3.3   Network Transport Services

Call Set Up Time

This is usually faster on a circuit-switched network: 100 milliseconds as compared with a few hundred milliseconds.

Types of Services

The services obtained on a packet network are usually the virtual circuit services. However, a few packet networks are offering the detagram service, which is the delivery of independent packets of information.

The circuit-switched network also offers port concentration services which are very useful for a time-sharing computer.

A packet-switching network allows large numbers of virtual circuits (up to 4,096 according to the X25 standard) to be multiplexed on a single physical port.

Many other services can be implemented on a network — e.g. closed user groups, hunt groups, autobaud, etc.

184

Speed conversion and protocol conversion can be more easily obtained on a packet network than on a circuit network.

Throughput with Respect to Bandwidth

In a circuit-switched network, the throughput is given by the bit rate of the virtual circuit. In a packet-switched network, the overhead on each packet reduces the throughput per virtual circuit. This can have a significant effect on batch or file transmissions.

Error Protection

Only the packet network offers error protection (through an error detection code and packet retransmission) as a normal service.

Protocol Conversion

The circuit-switched network does not usually offer protocol conversion facilities; in contrast, a packet switching network does offer protocol conversion facilities since: a) the store and forward technique used is well adapted to this task and b) the usual network DTE environment is heterogeneous in terms of protocols. Protocol conversion is often completed by some form of terminal control of transcoding (e.g. the ITT Fax Pak network which converts group one fax transmission into group two standard).

9.3.4 Economics

The relative advantages of packet versus circuit switching are dependent on the type of traffic handled by the network and its volumes. Furthermore, if the document transmission network is going to be shared by other types of traffic such as text transmission or computer data transmission, the relative advantages of packet versus circuit switching may be changed because of the traffic characteristics and the internode link capacity required.

In addition to Euronet, there are several other networks operating internationally in Europe whose performance and cost may be relevant to ARTEMIS.

The OECD published this year in its series on Information, Computer and Communications Policy a monograph entitled "The Usage of International Data Networks in Europe". Among the networks described are those operated by:

- CERN;
- COST — European Informatics Network;
- SWIFT;
- IIASA;

- NORDIC — Data Network;
- TRANSPAC;
- DATEX;
- RETD;
- EPSS — (UK network, now closed).

They also studied several private networks with annual traffic volumes of 0.4 to 60 x 10^{10} bits. The total cost per 1,000 characters was one to ten US cents for line costs. (The total data communications cost, including staff, terminals and so on, is typically twice the line rental.)

For ARTEMIS, handling ten million pages per annum with 10^{11} to 10^{12} bits, the range of cost on a private network should be similar — i.e. one to ten cents for a page of keystrokes, 20 cents to $2.00 for a page of facsimile.

If ARTEMIS uses the public networks, such as TRANSPAC in France and Euronet, internationally, the costs are respectively one to four cents and 20 to 80 cents for keystrokes and facsimile.

ARTEMIS may be able to establish a few "heavy duty" links moving 10^4 pages of facsimile, which is 2.10^9 bits, or more overnight — i.e. in 5.10^4 seconds. A 40K bps link would be needed, at a cost of, say, $3,000 per month. Such a link would carry 10^5 pages in 20 nights at a cost of 3 cents/page. This is an order of magnitude less than on a public switched network.

Size of the Network

This is critical in evaluating the benefit of a given switching/transmission technique. The main cost of a large network — say with more than 500 DTEs — is due to the tie lines, the interface cards and modems to connect the DTEs to the network.

A typical breakdown of costs for a data network is:

Internode trunk	$\simeq$	20 per cent of total network cost
Nodes	$\simeq$	20 per cent of total network cost
Terminal network connection cost	$\simeq$	60 per cent

A major conclusion is: the concentration technique used within the network is not critical provided it uses the transmission resources efficiently. As an example, using 20 per cent more trunk bandwidth would increase network cost by only four per cent.

Circuit switching is particularly well suited for fax transmission and efficient file transfer. Packet switching is particularly well suited for conversational traffic. However, use of T1 trunk (1.5 or 2M bps) for a packet switching network could improve its relative performance for fax and files.

186

General Economic Trends

The cost of computation is decreasing at a faster rate than that of transmission; therefore, it is worthwhile today, and should be even more so over the next few years, to invest in data handling in order to reduce bandwidth. This means in particular that packet switching technology is going to be improved and so will probably find new applications.

The tariff structure could have a strong impact on the selection of transmission technique. For example, as soon as a tariff is distance-independent, local data or information transfer is subsidising long distance transfer. Therefore, it might be more economical to have local transfers done via independent leased channels or via the telephone network.

The cost of a packet switching node is higher than that of a circuit switching node. The price of a basic terminal for a large network (more than 1,000 terminals) should be around $1,000–2,000 for a circuit-switched network and $2,000–3,000 for a packet network.

When designing a network, one should be ready to consider, even within the same network, different techniques which could be jointly used − e.g. multiplexing and data concentration, circuit switching and data concentration and even circuit switching and packet switching used in a hybrid network.

9.3.5   Packet Versus Circuit: A Summary

The key advantage of packet switching is multiplexing several sessions or dialogue on one single physical port. The main advantage of circuit switching is its protocol-independent transport function. However, the development of standards such as X25 and their adoption by the DP industry would counteract this advantage.

Bandwidth savings are normally achieved by using a packet rather than a circuit switching network. Bandwidth requirements are at least 50 per cent, (and may be up to 90 per cent) less for packet switching than for circuit switching.

There now exist many different types of off-the-shelf packet switching nodes (Transpac, Telenet, Datapac, French Railways, etc) while data circuit switching networks are less numerous (Siemens, Ericsson).

Many comparisons of packet and circuit networks have been made. It appears that packet switches are more expensive today than circuit switching nodes; a rough estimate gives a ratio of 2:1. However, one can expect to have, within five years, comparable prices for both types of switches.

A recent study by NAC (2) shows that the backbone network for the American Department of Defense would be more economical, using packet switching than circuit switching for a voice traffic of 2,700 erlangs and for a data traffic of 36 megabits. Another study made by Rosner (Computer Networks, North Holland, 1976, number 1) shows other economic advantages of packet switching.

Though packet switching is often more advantageous than circuit switching, one can use the following guideline:

> "If the average traffic flow per virtual circuit is of the order of one tenth or
> more of the trunk speed, then the effective statistical smoothing is not enough
> to really benefit from the packet switching technique. In these circumstances,
> a circuit switch network might offer a viable alternative".

If the number of terminals attached to the network is large compared with the number of hosts, the port concentration obtained using a packet network is clearly an advantage. If the number of terminals attached to the network is not large in comparison with the number of hosts, then this advantage becomes marginal.

There are switching nodes available today which offer the circuit switching service together with the multiplexing of very short packets on an end-to-end basis. The Tran Telecommunication Corporation equipment is a typical example. This type of equipment is generally more expensive than a packet node; however, it exhibits the advantages of both approaches.

When designing a network, one will have to specify the time frame of service of the network and the various types of traffic expected and the corresponding traffic matrices. It is then quite probable that different parts of the network may have sound economic reasons for using different transmission techniques. For example: point-to-point time multiplexed circuits between a few high traffic hosts and a packet network for the other hosts and terminals.

REFERENCES

1. Circuit and packet switching, "A Cost Performance Trade-Off Study", North Holland, Computer Networks Number 1, 1976 (7–26).

2. DOD Network Study by NAC. Dr Howard Frank and Dr Israel Gitman, (US Department of Commerce, National Technical Information Service), "Economic Analysis of Integrated DOD Voice and Data Networks". September 1978. AD/A–059 981.

3. Comparing Network Technologies, R.W. Sanders, Datamation, July 1978.

4. The Evolution of Packet Switching, L. G. Roberts, IEEE Proceedings, June 1978.

5. Packet Switching Networks Seek a Bigger Role, G. Burch, R. Gruber, Datacommunication, May/June 1976.

10.   SATELLITE COMMUNICATIONS FOR ARTEMIS

Contents

Summary

SUMMARY

It has been suggested that ARTEMIS should send full texts from its archives to printing centres by satellite. If ARTEMIS were to fulfil all requests in this way, about 100 million pages might be sent each year. Assuming that most pages were in facsimile rather than keystroke format, the total volume would be 2.10^{13} bits per annum, requiring a channel of two Mbits/second capacity. Since a single transponder can take 40 Mbits/second, ARTEMIS would share capacity with other users.

The cost of leasing a whole transponder might be about $1 million per annum, or one cent per page. Each printing centre would need a receiving aerial costing $100 to $1,000 per annum, which would be spread over 10,000 to ten million pages, at an average cost of less than one cent/page except at marginally viable centres.

Each ARTEMIS archive would need either a ground station of its own or a link to a shared transmitter, at a typical cost of $100,000 per annum. Assuming ten equal centres sending 100 million pages between them, each page costs about one cent.

The whole system would cost a few cents per page at a volume of 100 million pages going to about 1,000 centres, and the total cost would be about $2 million.

For much lower traffic, such as one million pages, the total cost would not drop proportionately and the page cost might rise towards $1.00. Euronet could deliver one million pages of facsimile for less than $1 million and even lower costs would be possible using the PSTN and leased data communications links.

10.1   Introduction

ARTEMIS might use a satellite transponder* as the only, or as an optional, means of communicating between its archives and its printing centres.

If ARTEMIS management has the authority and capability to decree how printing centres get their material, then it can choose to minimise the total cost of the system.   For satellite communications, this will include:

- Link to ground station for transmission;
- Transmitting aerials;
- Lease to transponder capacity;
- Receiving aerials.

If ARTEMIS printing centre managements individually select their means of reception of pages for printing, then they will seek to minimise their own total costs.   These will include, for satellites:

- Receiving aerials;
- Fees to ARTEMIS for use of satellite delivery service.

In the following chapters, we discuss first the economics for ARTEMIS as a whole, and then the viewpoint of an individual print centre.   Finally, we look at different ways in which ARTEMIS management might choose to spread the costs of transmission among the receiving print centres.

ARTEMIS will never create sufficient traffic to require a satellite of its own, or even a whole transponder.   A typical transponder provides 40.10^6 bits/second or about 10^{15} bits per annum. Even for facsimile, this provides almost 10^{10} pages per annum, enough to meet one milliard typical requests.   We expect ARTEMIS traffic to be two orders of magnitude less than this, with about ten million requests.   It follows that ARTEMIS will share a transponder and earth stations, probably using them at night.

European satellites which might provide such capacity to ARTEMIS, are described briefly below.

The ESA OTS, an experimental *fixed service* (see below) satellite, has been working successfully for a year.   OTS has been used by PTTs and broadcasters for numerous experiments and by France to relay a TV service to Tunisia.   The experiments include high speed data interchange between CERN in Geneva and Rutherford Laboratory in Oxford using a three-metre antenna.

---

*Readers unfamiliar with satellites will find an introduction in Annex B

ESA plans to launch two European Communications Satellites (ECS) in 1981 and 1982. ECS will have twice the capacity of OTS and will provide two video and 12,000 telephone channels. British Aerospace has proposed a version of ECS for Radio-Tele-Luxembourg (RTL) which could transmit to one-metre receiving antennae.

RTL has studies underway to clarify the technical, operational and financial variables involved in the supply and use of an RTL-dedicated satellite for the direct broadcast of RTL television programmes. Alternatively, RTL might lease capacity from French or German satellites.

France and Germany have agreed on a proposal for a joint system, initially comprising a satellite each, to broadcast on existing national TV channels. Since this requires, according to ITU allotment plans, only five channels per country, the remaining capacity is available for other purposes. The cost of the two satellites, their launchings and control systems, is estimated to be $350 million, and antennae are likely to retail for $550 each. The first may be operational by 1983.

France is also planning two national communications satellites, to be built by Matra for about $360 million and to be launched in 1982/1983. They will be used for TV and telephone links between mainland France and its overseas departments and for internal computer, teleconferencing, telecopier and telefacsimile services. A total of 300 users are expected to have their own direct antennae.

The British IBA has two satellite experiments, including a portable up-link with a 2.5 metre trailer-mounted dish antenna and a three-metre receiving terminal.

MARECS, for communications between ships and shore facilities, will use a satellite, due for launch this year.

Communications satellites are operated under a complicated legal regime. The ITU defines *services,* distinguishing 18 for frequency allotments. Fixed satellite service, broadcasting satellite service and mobile satellite service have different allotments but the technical distinctions are less clear than the regulatory ones. It is not clear whether ARTEMIS would use a broadcasting service frequency or a fixed service frequency to reach small dish antennae.

Because ARTEMIS will be so small a user that it cannot invest in its own satellite, its communications charges from a satellite operator will be determined by tariffs and by negotiation, not by the cost of providing a channel. In this paper, we have not tried to guess the outcome of any negotiation for, say, the use of a TV channel between midnight and dawn; instead, we have used an Intelsat tariff as an example.

Transmitting and receiving aerials are the focus of much research, with significant pioneering efforts being made in Canada. Experiments there have demonstrated 1.2 metre receive-only aerials for tunable reception from Anik-B which cost $2,500 now and may drop below $1,000 if

10,000 are produced. Single channel small receiving antennae may cost as little as $100 to $1,000.

The Canadians are also working on two-way limited capability earth stations for $30,000 or less, to replace today's five-metre aerials costing more than $200,000. Such transmitters might suit ARTEMIS eventually, but for its early operations, ARTEMIS would rent capacity on someone else's earth station for transmission. Again, we have not tried to forecast the rental that might be agreed.

10.2 Total System Cost of a Satellite Link

Let there be, as shown in Figure 10.2.A:

N   ARTEMIS stores

n   Receive-only print centres

B   Bits of information transmitted from stores to print centres per annum

b   Bits/second capacity of transponder.

Define the following unit costs in $ per annum:

G   Ground station and link to store

g   Receiver for print centre

T   Per bit/second capacity on transponder.

Then the total cost of transmission will be, in $ per annum:

$$NG + ng + bT$$

The cost per bit will be:

$$\frac{NG + ng + bT}{B}$$

Since there are 10^7 seconds in 250 nights of 11 hours:

$$B = 10^7 b \quad or \quad b = 10^{-7} B$$

Since there are 2.10^5 bits on a fax page and 10^{4*} on a page of keystrokes, the respective costs per page are, in cents:

$$\frac{NG + ng + BT \cdot 10^{-7}}{B} \cdot 2.10^7 \quad \text{(fax)}$$

$$\frac{NG + ng + BT \cdot 10^{-7}}{B} \cdot 10^6 \quad \text{(key)}$$

---

*Later analysis suggest this figure should be 1.6×10^4 since data compression will not be used

FIGURE 10.2.A

ARTEMIS SATELLITE COST ANALYSIS

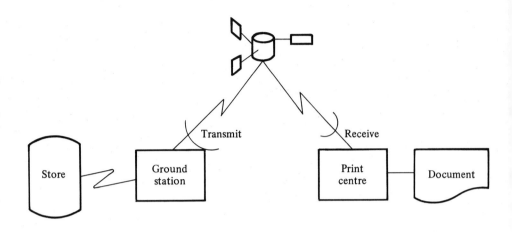

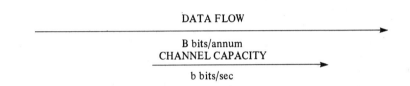

DATA FLOW

B bits/annum
CHANNEL CAPACITY

b bits/sec

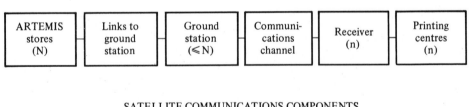

SATELLITE COMMUNICATIONS COMPONENTS

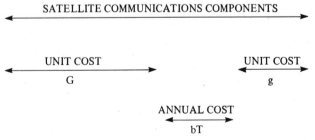

UNIT COST
G

UNIT COST
g

ANNUAL COST
bT

Simplifying, and using $|$ to denote "OR" for keystrokes and fax respectively, we get:

$$\left[\left(\frac{NG + ng}{B} \cdot 10^7 \right) + T \right] \left(10^{-1} \mid 2 \right)$$

Variant 1 — Base Case

For the base case, suppose:

B	=	10^{12}	bits/annum (10^8 $\mid$ 5.10^6 pages)
N	=	10	stores
n	=	10^3	printing centres
G	=	10^5	\$ per annum*
g	=	10^2	\$ per annum
T	=	10^{-2}	\$ per annum per bit/second

Then   NG = 10^6 \$ per annum
       ng = 10^5 \$ per annum

Using the mathematical symbols 0 ( ) to denote of the order of:

$$\left(\frac{NG + ng}{B} \right) \cdot 10^7 \ = \ 0 \ (10) \ \ \gg \ \ T$$

And the cost per page is one cent $|$ 20 cents.

In the base case, the cost is essentially:

$$\left(\frac{NG}{B} \right) \cdot 10^7 \cdot \left(10^{-1} \mid 2 \right)$$

We will now explore a series of variants, based on increasing or decreasing the number of locations and the traffic volumes and on different arrangements for hiring communications capacity and ground stations.

These variants are:

1)   The base case, already calculated.

2) $\dfrac{NG}{B}$ greater since B is lower — i.e. smaller volume.

---

*We have assumed an SBS-type ground station at \$350,000 capital cost, which has maintenance plus amortisation costs of \$100,000 per annum including any link between store and ground station

3)   NG declines or ng increases so that ng = *0* (NG)
        – i.e. cheaper transmission, numerous receivers.

4)   T is greater, reflecting higher tariffs, so:

$$\left(\frac{NG + ng}{B}\right) \cdot 10^7 = 0 \text{ (T)}$$

or because the left hand side of the equation also declines.

Variant 2

In this variant $\dfrac{NG}{B} \gg \dfrac{ng}{B} \gg 10^{-7} \text{ T}$

so the transmitting ground station costs for each page that is sent dominate the page cost.

If the communications cost per page is to be less than Euronet (50 cents at peak times for 10^5 bits), then:

$$\frac{NG}{B} \leqslant 50. \ 10^{-7} = 5.10^{-6}$$

In the base case, $\dfrac{NG}{B} = 10^{-6}$

$N = 10$ stores

$G = 10^5$ \$ per annum

$B = 10^{12}$ bits/annum or 5.10^6 pages of fax, so the average traffic through each store is half million pages per annum, (10,000 per week or 2,000 per night).

If a store has less traffic than will justify its own ground station, then it will send its pages via Euronet or more cheaply to another store for transmission. This happens for $G = 10^5$ \$ per annum when the traffic, B, is 2.10^{10} bits/annum, giving:

$$\frac{NG}{B} = \frac{1. \ 10^5}{2. \ 10^{10}} = 5.10^{-6}$$

So $\dfrac{N}{B} < 5.10^{-11}$

for all transmitting centres using a ground station costing as much as \$100,000 per annum. In other works, every centre transmitting 2.10^{10} bits/annum or more would spend \$100,000 on a ground station rather than use Euronet.

Note, however, that a leased line link to a neighbouring country with capacity 10^4 bits per second for 2.10^7 seconds each year – i.e. 2.10^{11} bits per annum – costs only $25,000 per annum. So we have the following decision table for an individual ARTEMIS centre.

CONDITION	ACTION		
Traffic (in bits per annum)	Own ground station	International leased line	Euronet
$> 8.10^{11}$	x		
$> 5.10^9$		x	
$< 5.10^9$			x

For low traffic volumes within the same country, where a 500 Kilometre leased line costs about 10^4 dollars (BPOC tariff T), the breakeven with Euronet is 2.10^9 pages.

Sending the traffic to a nearby ground station instead of using one's own does not increase ground station costs for the nearby centre since its capacity is so much higher than needed $\left(\sim 4.10^{14} \text{ bits/annum} \right)$.

ARTEMIS would rent capacity on the ground station of a non-ARTEMIS owner, only if the cost were less than owning its own, so $G \leqslant 10^5$ \$ per annum always.

Variant 3

The base case assumes $100 per annum for a rudimentary antenna at each of 1,000 print stations. This gives ng = 10^5 \$ per annum which is much less than NG. However, values of ng could rise so that ng $>$ NG and becomes the dominant cost.

Firstly, n could reach 100,000 for a very popular service, with an accompanying rise in B, so that the cost per page approaches:

$$\left(\frac{ng}{B}\right) \cdot 10^7 \cdot \left(10^{-1} \mid 2\right)$$

The printing centre would have to receive enough pages to justify its aerial, setting a lower limit for $\left(\frac{n}{B}\right)$ for a $100 per annum aerial of $\frac{1}{10^7}$. This assumes that 50 pages of facsimile (2.10^5 bits/page) at $2.00 per page for communications would be viable. Then B for n = 10^5 would be 10^{12} if all aerials were viable. In practice, we would expect the busiest ten per cent of receivers to take 90 per cent of the traffic, so the remaining 90 per cent (almost 10^5 aerials) carry only ten per cent. Therefore, B would have to be 10^{13} bits per annum, or 5.10^6 requests for fax, 10^8 for keystrokes. With 100,000 aerials, the cost of each would not be higher than $100 per annum. So, for a popular service, once again:

$$\left(\frac{ng}{B}\right) \cdot 10^7 \cdot \left(10^{-1} \mid 2\right) \longrightarrow 1 \text{ cent} \mid 20 \text{ cents per page}$$

Conversely, if n were as low as 10, g would rise, perhaps to $1,000 per annum. Most of the traffic would not go by satellite link, so B would drop, perhaps to 5.10^4 pages for fax or 10^6 of keystrokes. Then, yet again:

$$\left(\frac{ng}{B}\right) \cdot 10^7 \cdot \left(10^{-1} \mid 2\right) \longrightarrow 1 \text{ cent} \mid 20 \text{ cents per page}$$

With $B = 10^{13}$, and lots of cheap receiving aerials, NG < ng if NG < 10^7, or N < 10^2. Since every transmitting ground station must have at least 8.10^{11} bits, N ⩽ 12 for $B = 10^{13}$. So NG < ng if $B = 10^{13}$ and ng = 10^7.

However, if ng = 10^4 and $B = 10^{10}$, then NG > ng even for one ground station at 10^5 $ per annum.

It is revealing to rearrange the expression for the cost of a page as follows:

$$\left(\frac{NG + ng}{B}\right) \cdot 10^7 \cdot \left(10^{-1} \mid 2\right)$$

$$= \frac{1 + \left(\frac{n}{N} \cdot \frac{g}{G}\right)}{\left(B/N\right)} \cdot 10^7 \cdot G \cdot \left(10^{-1} \mid 2\right)$$

This is the form which reflects expensive ground stations, G $\sim 10^5$ $ per annum, and

$$\left(\frac{n}{N}\right) \cdot \left(\frac{g}{G}\right) \ll 1.$$ To get below 20 cents per page of fax, B/N > 10^{11} is required. However, B/n > 10^{12}, otherwise a leased line would be used. So if a satellite were used, then the cost would be one cent/page or less for transmission.

Rearranging again, we get the cost per page in the form:

$$\frac{1 + \left(\frac{N}{n} \cdot \frac{G}{g}\right)}{\left(B/n\right)} \cdot 10^7 \cdot g \cdot \left(10^{-1} \mid 2\right)$$

If the ground station is subsidised or shared so that $\left(\dfrac{N}{n}\right) \cdot \left(\dfrac{G}{g}\right) \ll 1$, then recipients get pages of facsimile at 20 cents or less if they receive 1,000 pages per year.

Variant 4

The ground equipment for transmission and reception cost per page is:

$$\left(\frac{NG + ng}{B}\right) \cdot 10^7 \cdot \left(10^{-1} \mid 2\right)$$

We have shown that, in the base case:

$$\left(\frac{NG + ng}{B}\right) \cdot 10^7 = 0\,(10)$$

For the transmission cost to be dominant in the cost per page, we require:

$$\left(\frac{bT}{B}\right) > \left(\frac{NG + ng}{B}\right)$$

In the base case:

$$\left(\frac{bT}{B}\right) = \left(\frac{b}{B}\right) \cdot T = 10^{-7}\,T$$

and $\left(\dfrac{NG + ng}{B}\right) \gtrsim 10^{-6}$

However, we can conceive of conditions, such as free loan of a transmitting ground station, where:

$$NG < ng$$

and $\left(\dfrac{ng}{B}\right) = 0\,(10^{-5})$

This happens for $g = \$100$ and $(n/B) = 10^{-7}$, or $g = \$1,000$ and $(n/B) = 10^{-8}$.

So for transmission costs to dominate:

$$10^{-7} \cdot T > 10^{-5}$$

or $\qquad T > 10^2$

The cost of leasing an INTELSAT pre-emptible global beam transponder was $1 million per annum in 1977 for a capacity of 40 Mb/second, which is almost 10^{14} bits/annum. (However, the cost of leasing a TV channel on a European satellite is quoted* as $44 million per annum.)

ARTEMIS would find it worthwhile to lease a whole transponder if it could send 2.10^5 bits for 20 cents, which is 10^{12} bits for $1 million. So for high volumes:

$$T \; < \; \frac{\$10^6}{10^{12} \text{ bits}/2.10^7 \text{ seconds}} \;\; = \;\; \frac{2.10^{13}}{10^{12}} \;\; = \;\; 20$$

So above 10^{12} bits/annum, $T < 10^2$, and ground costs dominate the space segment.

Below 10^{12} bits/annum, ARTEMIS management would have to negotiate for part of the capacity of a transponder, which might be a channel available all the time, or all the transponder for part of the night. We showed in Variant 2 that below 8.10^{11} bits, it would be cheaper for any centre to use a leased line to the nearest ground station rather than have its own. So if there are only 10^{12} bits/annum, there will be at most one ground station and a few hundred receiving antennae.

If ARTEMIS could use one per cent of the capacity for less than ten per cent of the cost ($P per annum) of a transponder, the cost per page of fax would be:

$$\frac{NG + ng + P}{B} \; \cdot \; 2.10^7 \; = \; \frac{10^5 + 10^5 + 10^5}{10^{12}} \cdot 2.10^7 \; = \; 6 \text{ cents}$$

*Intermedia, January 1980, Volume 8, Number 1, page 8

CONCLUSION

Suppose ARTEMIS has to invest in at least one ground station and lease a transponder, at a total cost of $1.1 x 10^6 per annum, in order to use satellite communications. Then if it has just one fulfilment centre operating at 10^{12} bits per annum, the cost of sending a page of fax will be about 20 cents.

As the total volume rises above 10^{12} bits per annum, each centre will invest in its own ground station as it approaches 10^{12} bits per annum. The cost per page will stay at or below 20 cents, and decline further as the ground station and transmission costs are spread over yet more traffic.

At 10^{14} bits per annum, representing 50 million requests for ten pages of facsimile each year, the ground station and transponder would cost $10 million (which is two cents per page) or less. (If there were 100 centres averaging 10^{12} bits, many would not have ground stations of their own; in practice, they might share about ten stations, using 90 national leased lines to centres without ground stations, at a total cost of much less than $3 million. Ninety national leased lines cannot cost more than $750,000 at BPOC tariff T rates.)

The total cost of receivers exceeds that of transmitters plus space segment when 1,000 are installed and the total traffic exceeds 10^{12} bits per annum. With an average traffic of 10,000 pages of facsimile, each page costs one cent.

At lower volumes than 10^{12} bits/annum, ARTEMIS may be able to negotiate to share a single ground station and transponder, so that the cost stays below 20 cents per page for sending facsimile.

For example, at 10^{10} bits/annum, 20 cents per page of 2.10^5 bits provides $10,000 from 50,000 pages. If a viable receiver requires at least 200 pages per annum (to undercut Euronet), and ten per cent of receivers have 90 per cent of the traffic, there will be only 50 receivers in operation. The transmission volumes would only justify one ARTEMIS store, which would have to be sited near the ground station. Even then, it would probably be less trouble to pay Euronet 50 cents per page — i.e. $50,000 per annum — than try to use the satellite.

However, at 10^{11} bits per annum, Euronet would cost $500,000 and there would be a possible $100,000 for the space segment. There might be 500 viable receivers, of which 50 receive almost one million pages between them. One store would be near the ground station, and, say, three others would link to it by leased lines at a cost of $75,000. $25,000 might be sufficient to rent the ground station and a channel each night.

10.3   Incremental Cost of Adding a Printing Centre

Suppose each printing centre can choose how to connect to ARTEMIS and has the following options:

- Satellite aerial at $100 per annum;
- Euronet at 50 cents per page;
- Dial-up line to nearest multiplexer at 1,200 bps;
- Leased line to nearest multiplexer.

Then volume and distance determine the choice, assuming that each centre has appropriate terminals and modems already.

In the figures on the next two pages, 10.3.A and 10.3.B, we show the approximate costs per page of different methods at two representative distances for a range of volumes.

The almost horizontal lines, Euronet and the public switched telephone network (PSTN), both have volume-related charges.   It is evident that Euronet for inland as opposed to international calls is always more expensive.

The Euronet tariff for the UK at cheap rates is shown in Table 10.3.A with examples.   Small users would pay 60 cents per facsimile page at cheap rates but nearer 90 cents during the day. Large users would be nearer 55 cents and 85 cents respectively.   Euronet ignores both distance and international borders and is cheaper than the PSTN for any international data communications.   Both Euronet and the PSTN require for data transmission suitable modems which would be expensive for small users who did not need them for other applications.   However, small users would couple their fax receiver's built-in modem directly to the line, not use a separate modem.

The following table shows BPOC charges for cheap rate inland and international telephone calls in 1979 and the corresponding cost for fax at 2,400 bps:

Distance	Seconds for £0.03 (6.6 US cents)	US cents for 2.10^5 bits (approximate)
Inland		
Local	720	1
< 56 Kilometres	180	4
> 56 Kilometres	60	12
Abroad		
Netherlands	9.6	60
Austria	8	80
Greece	6	100
USA	3.2	200
Saudi Arabia	2.4	240
India	1.7	340

FIGURE 10.3.A

TRANSMISSION COSTS FOR PRINTING CENTRES
(at a range of 100 kilometres)

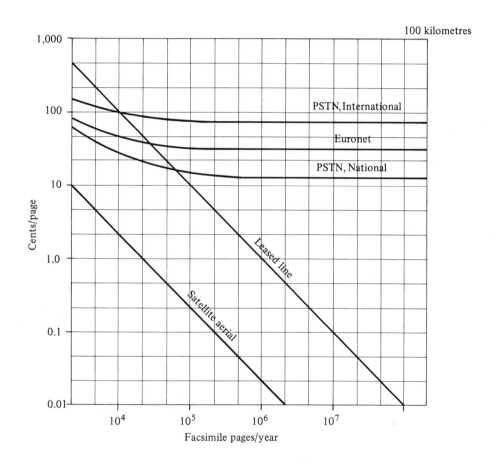

FIGURE 10.3.B

TRANSMISSION COSTS FOR PRINTING CENTRES
(at a range of 10 kilometres)

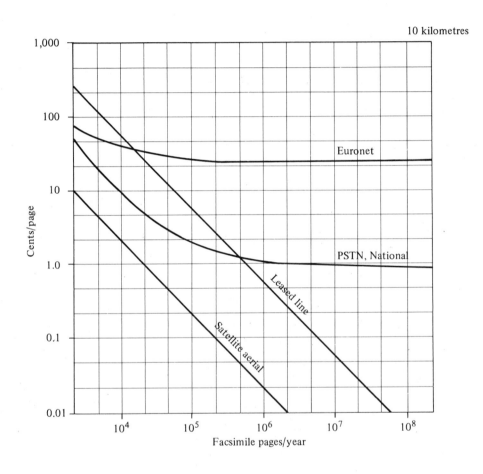

TABLE 10.3.A

EURONET TARIFF, UK, CHEAP RATE

		Leased lines	Dial-up
Once only charges		£150	£25
Annual rental	— 1,200 bps	£143.75	£20
	— 9,600 bps	£200.00	
Duration	— 1,200 bps	1.4p/min	1.8p/min
	— 9,600 bps	1.8p/min	
Volume	— per 10,000 bits	1.56p	1.56p

Examples

1. **Large users at 9,600 bps, requesting ten pages of facsimile (2.10^6 bits), 10,000 times per page:**

		Per page	
		Pence	ECU
Annual cost per page £200 + £150 x 20%* over 100,000	=	0.23	0.035
Duration cost at 20 seconds/page	=	0.6	0.092
Volume cost	=	26.0	0.400
TOTAL	=	26.83	0.527

2. **Small user dialling in at 1,200 bps, requesting ten pages of keystrokes (1.4×10^5 bits), 100 times per year:**

		Per page	
		Pence	ECU
Annual cost per page £20 + £25 x 20%* over 1,000	=	2.5	0.038
Duration cost at 140 seconds/page	=	4.2	0.065
Phone call charge at 24 minutes/6p	=	0.6	0.009
Volume cost	=	1.8	0.028
TOTAL	=	9.1	0.140

*Amortisation over five years

A leased line has a fixed annual cost which varies with distance. It requires a modem at each end. The BPOC tariff for a suitable link is shown in Figure 10.3.C and Table 10.3.B. Modems of 9,600 bps capacity can be substituted at higher cost. In Figures 10.3.A and 10.3.B, we have used total costs of $5,000 at 100 kilometres and $2,500 at 10 kilometres. On such lines, 30 cents per page is achieved at annual volumes of ~ 17,000 pages and ~ 8,500 pages respectively.

Because of the high cost of modems, even a $1,000 per annum disk aerial for satellite reception is cheaper than a leased line of any length in Britain. (This is why Viewdata sets have to have built-in modems in the UK.) It is possible that ARTEMIS aerials can be as cheap as $100 per annum and will need no expensive interface between dish and printing centre.

It follows that a high volume user will choose a dish aerial under all conditions if he has to pay only for installation of the receiver; below a critical volume, which will depend on distance, he will use the PSTN.

Modems

If the print centres connect to ARTEMIS archives over leased lines or the public switched telephone network for data communications, they will generally require modems. At very low volumes, they may use an acoustic coupler. Facsimile machines have their modems built in, and so do Viewdata sets. Most modems are provided by PTTs to CCITT standards.

The BPOC tariff for a modem 12 for use on the Datel service, on leased or dial-up lines respectively, is:

Annual rental £330 or £380	$720 or $835
Connection charge £120	$265

Spreading the connection charge over five years, the total cost is about $795 or $890 per annum per modem.

A leased line connection requires two modems but a dial up link would share the distant modem, so only requires one at the printing centre. A leased line (or dial-up) connection to Euronet also requires two (or one) modems. (See Figure 10.3.D.)

Print centres may be able to spread the cost of modems over many applications, including ARTEMIS, thus greatly reducing costs.

It should be noted that modem tariffs are very high compared with modem costs. In Datamation's survey, March 1979, medium-speed modems in America had purchase prices mainly between $400 and $1,000, although Bell's data set 201A costs $800 (DDD) or $660 (leased line) per annum.

FIGURE 10.3.C

BPOC TARIFF T (SMOOTHED)
WITH PO MODEMS-12

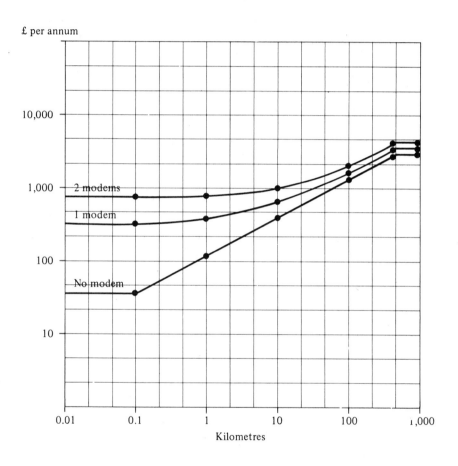

£ per annum

Kilometres

TABLE 10.3.B

BPOC TARIFF T

This specification is designed primarily for non-speech (e.g. data transmission or facsimile). It is generally used at 1,200 bps with a PO modem at each end.

Costs in £s, March 1978

Distance (km)	Connection charges		Annual rental		TOTAL	
	Line	Modem	Line	Modem	Line	Line + 2 modems
0.1	20	120	34	330	38	766
1	40	120	103	330	111	815
10	40	120	395	330	403	1,107
100	90	120	1,580	330	1,598	2,402
1,000*	120	120	3,890	330	3,914	4,618

*Above 480 kilometres, the tariff is constant

FIGURE 10.3.D

PRINT CENTRE CONNECTION TO ARTEMIS

	Home modem	Time charge	Leased line	Distant modem	Euronet charge	Cost of antenna
Leased line Direct to ARTEMIS	X		X	X		
Dial-up line Direct to ARTEMIS	X	X				
Leased line Via Euronet	X		X	X	X	
Dial-up line Via Euronet	X	X			X	
Receive direct From Satellite						X

In all, 50 suppliers offered 400 models, covering the following range:

- Low-speed modems (to 600 bps),
- Medium-speed modems (to 2,400 bps),
- High-speed modems (to 9,600 bps);
- Wide-band modems (over 9,600 bps);
- Short-haul modems;
- Modem eliminators or line drivers;
- Telephone couplers;
- Parallel interface modems.

The proliferation results from the "Carterfone decision" by the FCC which allowed foreign attachments like independent modems to be connected to the dial-up network.

If ARTEMIS print centres could pay US prices, the cost of modems might be about $100 to $200 per year, which compares with $800 for common carrier supplied modems. Even in the USA, however, a modem might cost more than a small antenna.

Recovering Transmission Costs

If users choose dish aerials, ARTEMIS stores will somehow have to recover the cost of transmission. This could be done in the form of annual licence fees, which would increase the effective cost of aerials, or by levying a page charge.

In the former case, the licence could cost just less than two modems, without causing the user to install a leased line. However, this would encourage small print centres to use the PSTN instead of an antenna for up to perhaps 100,000 pages. So ARTEMIS would get fees from fewer aerials to pay the cost of broadcasting to them.

Alternatively, a page charge of, say, 20 cents for facsimile and one cent for keystrokes, irrespective of medium of delivery, would provide revenue of $1 per 10^6 bits or $1 million per annum at 10^{12} bits per annum. This should be enough to pay for a ground station and transponder.

ANNEX A

Conversion Figures

One Year	—	250 nights	—	10^7 seconds
One Night	—	12 hours	—	4.10^4 seconds
One Page	—	2.10^5 bits (fax)		
	—	1.6×10^4 bits (text)		
One request averages ten pages	=	2.10^6 bits (fax) after compression		
	=	1.6×10^5 bits (char) without compression		
One million requests per annum	=	10^7 pages in 10^7 seconds		
	=	1 page per second		

GLOSSARY

Analogue transmission Transmission of a continuously variable signal as opposed to a discretely variable signal. Physical quantities such as temperature are continuously variable and so are described as 'analogue'. Data characters, on the other hand, are coded in discrete separate pulses or signal levels, and are referred to as 'digital'.

Antiope — (see under Videotex)

Bit — Contraction of 'binary digit', the smallest unit of information in a binary system. A bit represents the choice between a mark or space (one or zero) condition.

Bit-stream and bit-string When a set of related bits — a bit-string — travels along a communications line, it forms a bit-stream.

bps Bits per second.

Black-box An electronic device which transforms an input signal into an output signal.

Bildschirm text (see under Videotex)

CCITT Consultative Committee on International Telegraphy and Telephony.

Conduit and content The distinction is drawn between the content of a message, which is the information it contains, and the conduit or medium on which the message travels.

Character recognition and character readers (see under OCR)

Character string A set of related characters, digits, punctuation signs and control codes, forming all or part of a message to be stored or transmitted.

Compaction and compaction algorithm The information in a bit-string can be recoded into fewer bits — i.e. a more compact form — by a compaction algorithm. (An algorithm is a rigorous mathematical procedure involving a sequence of steps.) All the information can be recovered with a complementary algorithm which recreates the original form. Compressing — expanding is contracted to *companding*.

219

Companding	(see under compaction)
CEPT	European Conference of Postal and Telecommunications Administrations.
Digitalise	Convert to digital data; (see under analogue transmission).
ECS	European Communications Satellite.
ECU	European Currency Unit The conversion rates at the beginning of 1980 were approximately:

Belgian Franc	40.4	French Franc	5.83
German Mark	2.49	Dutch Florin	2.75
British Pound	0.64	Irish Pound	0.67
Danish Kroner	7.76	Italian Lira	1,160
US Dollar	1.45	Canadian Dollar	1.70

Facsimile or Fax	A system for the transmission of images. The image is scanned at the transmitter, reconstructed at the receiving station and reproduced on some form of paper or microform.
Host	A computer system which performs the actual processing of data, such as those on a data base supplied by an *information provider* (q.v.). Hosts are attached to communications networks, over which they send messages, including the content of documents, for example, to users.
Index	(see under location index, subject index)
Information provider	The owner of information, or the owner's agent, who provides information to be stored in a data base on a host for delivery to users.
ISO	International Standards Organisation
Interface	A boundary between two pieces of equipment across which all signals that pass are accurately defined.
Journal	(see Librarians' glossary, below)

Librarian's glossary

The following terms are taken from 'The Librarian's Glossary of terms used in librarianship, documentation and the book craft' Harrod, L.M., 4th revised edition, 1977, published by Deutsch.

Journal

A newspaper or periodical. Particularly a periodical issued by a society or institution and containing news, proceedings, transactions and reports of work carried out in a particular field.

Book

At a UNESCO conference in 1964 a book was defined as 'a non-periodical printed publication of at least 49 pages, exclusive of cover pages'. See also Pamphlet.

Magazine

A periodical publication as distinct from a newspaper, separate issues being independently paginated and identified by date rather than by serial number.

Monograph

A separate treatise on a single subject or class of subjects, or on one person, usually detailed in treatment but not extensive in scope and often containing extensive bibliographies. Frequently published in series. In cataloguing, any publication which is not a Serial (q.v.).

Monograph Series

A series of monographs with a series title as well as individual titles; often issued by a university or society. See also Series.

Pamphlet

A non-periodical publication of at least five but not more than 48 pages, exclusive of the cover pages. (General Conference of UNESCO, 1964). See also Book. It usually has an independent entity, not being a Serial (q.v.), but it may be one of a series of publications having a similarity of format or subject matter.

Periodical	A publication with a distinctive title which appears at stated or regular intervals, generally oftener than once a year, without prior decision as to when the last issue shall appear. It contains articles, stories or other writings, by several contributors. Newspapers, whose chief function is to disseminate news, and the memoirs, proceedings, journals, etc. of societies are not considered periodicals under the cataloguing rules. See also Serial. At the General Conference of UNESCO, held at Paris on 19th November 1964, it was agreed that a publication is a periodical 'if it constitutes one issue in a continuous series under the same title, published at regular or irregular intervals, over an indefinite period, individual issues in the series being numbered consecutively or each issue being dated'. In statistical records, a periodical publication with a single system of numeration whether or not the title has changed. Where a change of numeration occurs, a new sequence starting at one, irrespective of any change of title, is considered to be a separate unit.
Serial	Any publication issued in successive parts, appearing at intervals, usually regular ones, and, as a rule, intended to be continued indefinitely. The term includes periodicals, newspapers, annuals, numbered monographic series and the proceedings, transactions and memoirs of societies. Not to be confused with Series (q.v.).
Series	Volumes usually related to each other in subject matter, issued successively, sometimes at the same price, and generally by the same publisher, in a uniform style, and usually bearing a collective 'series title' on the Half Title or the cover, or at the head of the Title-page.

Location Index	A computer file index which indicates the data base in which a digitalised document is located. (Contrast a *subject index*, q.v. below).
Monograph	(see Librarians' Glossary)
Modem	The device which accepts a digital wave form and adapts it for transmission over an analogue channel, such as a telephone circuit provides, and also receives signals from a distant modem and converts them back to digital form. A contraction of 'modulator-demodulator', but a modem contains more than this.
Mega	(see under units − SI)
MHC	Modified Huffman Coding ... a compaction algorithm for facsimile bit-strings which had been proposed as the CCITT Group 3 facsimile standard.
Micro	(see under units − SI)
Microform	Microfiche, microfilm or other photographically reduced document.
Multiplexer	Equipment which takes a number of communication channels and combines the signals into one common channel in such a way that the original signals can be extracted again by a demultiplexer.
Node	In a topological description of a network, a node is a point of junction of the links. The word has also come to mean a switching centre in the context of data networks, particularly in the context of packet switching.
OCR	Optical character recognition: a method of reading letters, digits and punctuation marks from documents into computers by recognising their shapes.
OTS	Orbital Test Satellite
Packet	A block of data handled by a network in a well defined format including a heading.

Packet Switching Network	A network designed to carry data in the form of packets (q.v.).
Prestel	(see under Videotex)
Protocol	A strict procedure required to initiate and maintain communication.
PSDN	Public switched data network.
PSN	Public switched network.
PSTN	Public switched telephone network.
SBS	Satellite Business Systems — an American corporation formed by IBM, Comsat General and Aetna to provide digital communications services at high speed via satellite to large corporations within the United States.
Spinner	Someone who 'spins off' works, generally in printed form, by computer processing from selected portions of machine readable data bases.
Subject index	An index used for finding documents by reference to their subject matter.
Tera	(see under units — SI)
Teletex	An improved telex-type service operating at higher speed and with a more extensive character set.
Units — SI	The International System of Units

The following table gives the names, symbols and equivalents of prefixes used in the international system to indicate multiples and sub-multiples of the units

Name	Symbol	Equivalent
Tera	T	10^{12}
Giga	G	10^{9}
Mega	M	10^{6}
Kilo	k	10^{3}
Hecto	h	10^{2}
Deca	—	10
Deci	d	10^{-1}

Name	Symbol	Equivalent
Centi	c	10^{-2}
Milli	m	10^{-3}
Micro	μ	10^{-6}
Nano	n	10^{-9}
Pico	p	10^{-12}

Videotex

The generic name used for electronic systems that use a modified TV set to display computer-based information. Interactive systems using, typically, the TV set and telephone line, are called telephone-based or *interactive* videotex. Broadcast services are called broadcast videotex, or *teletext*.

Viewdata	is the British generic term for interactive videotex.
Prestel	is the British Post Office's viewdata service.
Bildschirmtext	is the West German Bundespost's interactive videotex service.
Teletel	is the French interactive videotex service.
Antiope	is a French teletext system.

Other Titles from Knowledge Industry Publications

**Guide to Electronic Publishing: Opportunities in Online and
Viewdata Services**
by Fran Spigai and Peter Sommer
LC 81-20787   ISBN 0-914236-87-3 $95.00

U.S. Book Publishing Yearbook and Directory, 1981-82
edited by Judith S. Duke
LC 79-649219   ISBN 0-914236-99-7 $60.00

**Who Owns the Media? Concentration of Ownership in the Mass
Communications Industry**
edited by Benjamin M. Compaine
LC 79-15891   ISBN 0-914236-36-9 $24.95

The Library and Information Manager's Guide to Online Services
edited by Ryan E. Hoover
LC 80-21602   ISBN 0-914236-60-1 (cl) $29.50
                               ISBN 0-914236-52-0 (pbk) $24.50

Video Discs: The Technology, the Applications and the Future
by Efrem Sigel, Mark Schubin, and Paul F. Merrill, et al.
LC 80-23112   ISBN 0-914236-56-3 $29.95

**Videotext: The Coming Revolution in Home/Office Information
Retrieval**
edited by Efrem Sigel
LC 79-18935   ISBN 0-914236-41-5 $24.95

Electronic Mail: A Revolution in Business Communications
by Stephen Connell and Ian A. Galbraith
                               ISBN 0-86729-015-3 (cl) $32.95
                               ISBN 0-86729-016-1 (pbk) $22.95